Real People, Real Christmas:

Thirty-One Days Discovering the Hidden Treasures of the Christmas Story

Bo Jackson

DEDICATION

This book is dedicated to my amazingly cute Grandkids: Maddie, Gabe, Bo, Jase, Caleb, and Sullivan. You refresh Christmas for me every year with your faith and your joy! I love being your Papaw and I hope that the true message of Christmas will live forever in your hearts!

Copyright © 2018 Bo Jackson
All rights reserved.
ISBN: 9781729034910
ISBN-13:

CONTENTS

ACKNOWLEDGMENTS

All Scriptures are taken from BibleGateway.com,
or from the NIV Study Bible, Kenneth Barker, Editor,
Zondervan Bible Publishers, Grand Rapids, MI.
Cover pictures *Rest on the Flight into Egypt* by Luc-Olivier Merson and
Herod on His Throne by Théophile Marie François Lybaert used
from public domain

The Heartbeat of Christmas

December 1 A Love Story Like No Other

Luke 2:1 "And it came to pass in those days that a decree went out from Caesar Augustus that all the world should be registered. **2** This census first took place while Quirinius was governing Syria. **3** So all went to be registered, everyone to his own city.
4 Joseph also went up from Galilee, out of the city of Nazareth, into Judea, to the city of David, which is called Bethlehem, because he was of the house and lineage of David, **5** to be registered with Mary, his betrothed wife, who was with child. **6** So it was, that while they were there, the days were completed for her to be delivered. **7** And she brought forth her firstborn Son, and wrapped Him in swaddling clothes, and laid Him in a manger, because there was no room for them in the inn."
Paul McCartney wrote a song that said, "You'd think that people would have had enough of silly love songs; I look around me and I see it isn't so. Some people want to fill the world with silly love songs; Well, what's wrong with that? I'd like to know, 'cause here I go... again!" As I sit before my computer, poised to embark on a book about the Nativity, I am struck by the fact that the same thing could be said about Christmas: there are enough books on the subject to fill a library, and here is another one! So, why this book?
Christmas is surrounded by tradition and myth, by festivals and Holy Days, and it is imbedded in cultures around the world as a time to give gifts and commemorate the birth of Christ. It is portrayed in pageants and programs, celebrated with songs and services, and wrapped with more tradition than any gift under the Christmas tree. While most people still connect it with church, the heart-beat of Christmas is often muffled by culture and more recent traditions.
The commercialization of Christmas has added yet another layer to its lore, while the Christmas industry pumps billions through retailers from "black Friday" though Christmas Eve. We are bombarded with advertising, once-a-year sales, and recommendations for the perfect gift, all of which have very little to do with the event that got the whole Christmas thing started in the first place.
It's not just retailers who have hijacked the original Christmas story. The few quaint Christmas movies I saw growing up in the 60's (like "It's A Wonderful Life", "White Christmas", "Miracle on 34th Street", and "A Christmas Carol") have exploded into dozens of films vying for Holiday viewing, and there are a LOT of good ones! Added to "Frosty the Snowman" and "A Charlie Brown Christmas" are pithier, more modern stories, such "Christmas Vacation", "Home Alone", "A Christmas Story", "Elf", "Scrooged", "Christmas with the Kranks", and "Die Hard". And I'll admit it, I love watching most of them! But the net effect of all of these entertaining stories is that they have added yet another layer to Christmas that often has very little to do with the Reason for the Season.

At times our family has done an Advent calendar, which has little doors you open up every day from the first Sunday of Advent (usually between November 27th and December 3rd) until Christmas. (Some reusable calendars just start December 1st.) Behind each door you find a small treat of some kind, perhaps candy or chocolate. Advent calendars can be simple and made of paper, or they can be quite ornate and made of wood or ceramic so that they can be used for more than one season. Advent is a liturgical season celebrated by Christians of all denominations to bring focus upon the *adventus*, or coming of the Christ. Advent calendars offer a great way to anticipate the birth of Christ daily as the celebration of his birth approaches.

This book is an Advent Calendar for your mind, with devotions designed to bring focus upon the real reason for Christmas. It's not a narrative, or the Christmas story told the way you see it in pageants, but it is based on some observations that I think everyone should understand about the birth of Jesus:

1) It is Biblical. The Bible is full of references to the birth of the Messiah that surface not just in the Gospels, but throughout the Old Testament as well. It is amazing to look at the prophecies written hundreds of years before in the Biblical record of the birth of Jesus and connect the dots.

2) It is historical. There is **no doubt** that Jesus of Nazareth was born in Judea, lived in Galilee, and was crucified. It is very important to remember that Jesus was not mythological or fictional; you can perhaps argue that he was not who he said he was, but it's impossible to argue that he was never born.

3) It is a story full of gritty reality. More than tradition or Santa Claus, Christmas is the story of real people who lived in a dirty, dangerous world. It involves scandal, teenage pregnancy, international politics, a murderous king, and fugitives on the run from danger. It's history worth reading; it's reality worth remembering.

4) Finally, to bring us back to Paul McCartney, the birth of Jesus is important because it's a love story. There are love stories imbedded in the genealogies of Jesus; there is the love between Joseph and Mary, who navigated some incredibly difficult times together to remain faithful and to raise their family; and there is the Love of God, who sent his Son amid "good tidings of great joy, which shall be to all people."

As you read this, remember that **you** are one of those people, and that, while God's love story has been written for everyone, it's also been written just for **you**. I think you'll like the ending.

Jackson Family Christmas, 2017

Family pictures are full of smiles,
They're all about wearing appropriate styles,
With colors that match, a photographer there—
Everybody say cheese! Look up here! How's my hair?
A picture's a moment that's frozen in time,
Sent out with a card and a Holiday rhyme,
But there's more to each picture than anyone sees
Than the pose and the clothes and the light and the trees...
It's the story of us. It's the stories unseen
Of the work; of support; of just living the dream!
It contains all the conflicts, the pain and rejection,
A mother's fierce love, or a father's protection.
A family has jokes no one else seems to get;
It also has hurts that are hard to forget...
But a family remembers the good times we've had,
Like driving in Dumas, dress shopping with Dad,
Colorado adventures from now and back then;
It's riding a pony around on Long Glen!
It's that song that we sang; it's that bully who shoved you,
The places we lived; it's the mother who loved you!
A family's concussions, and stitches, and scars,
An assortment of various errors in cars,
And mistakes that a band-aid just couldn't erase:
It's a story of love and forgiveness and grace.
That picture can't tell all the secrets untold,

But I'll tell you **this**: this portrait is gold,
With a story behind every smile, every rhyme:
It's a precious mosaic that's frozen in time.
It's Mamaw and Papaw with kids in the park,
It's super cute Grandkids who love to play shark!
New jobs! New promotions! Our kids with careers!
It's Caleb and Sulli arriving to cheers!
Our family is growing in every way,
So we sent this Holiday picture to say,
We're grateful indeed for the way we've been blessed!
We hope that **your** Christmas is better than best!
Remember that Christ is how Christmas must start,
And enjoy CHRISTmas every day in your heart!

2 The Beginning

December 2   Ordinary People. An Extraordinary Genealogy

"This is the genealogy of Jesus the Messiah the son of David, the son of Abraham" (Matthew 1:1, NIV) Matthew (also known as Levi, the former tax collector) begins his biography of Jesus in a logical Hebrew fashion: he recounts his genealogy. This makes sense because patriarchal lineage was incredibly important in Israel, and every schoolboy could tell you who his father's father's father was, going back through multiple generations. In Matthew's genealogy of Jesus, however, there is something very surprising. Read it and see if it stands out to you: "Judah the father of Perez and Zerah, whose mother was Tamar... Salmon the father of Boaz, whose mother was Rahab, Boaz the father of Obed, whose mother was Ruth, Obed the father of Jesse, and Jesse the father of King David. David was the father of Solomon, whose mother (Bathsheba) had been Uriah's wife..." (Matthew 1:3, 5-6 NIV)

What do Tamar, Rahab, Ruth, Bathsheba, and Mary have in common? If you read Matthew 1, you'll find they are the only women mentioned in the genealogy of Jesus. Wow, only five women in that long list! That stands out for the nature of this list. It's not an aberration that there were so **few**, what is remarkable is that a Jewish genealogy mentioned ANY.

Luke's genealogy doesn't mention females. Hebrew family trees were usually only traced back through the fathers, so they did not normally include any women. Matthew, whose gospel was written primarily for a Jewish audience, presented Jesus as the Messiah who had been foretold in the Scriptures, as the promised King who would lead Israel... Yet he departs from Hebrew tradition in the opening stanza of his narrative!

It might be instructive to look at their stories and ask, why does Matthew include females in a patriarchal list that would normally be populated only by men? Why do these women stand out? Why are they mentioned specifically and centrally in the most amazing story within the best-selling book of all time? Why are these women, who were normally marginalized and relegated to the kitchen in ancient Middle Eastern culture, placed upon center stage in Matthew's Jewish gospel?

As we enter the season of Advent, it is worthwhile to consider the circumstances around the birth of Jesus. Matthew's unique introduction gives us something to ponder as we look at the arrival of the baby whose birth in an obscure place in a relatively primitive time has absolutely changed all of human history. As you read the story of Jesus, never forget that God often chooses unlikely and little-known candidates to change history. Never forget that the next candidate might be YOU.

Matthew's Genealogy of Jesus

The mystery of history is that the genealogy
Of Jesus out of Galilee defied conventionality,
The cultural philosophy, and practice of philology.
Matthew's careful document somehow put several women in it!
The genealogy was bent, a thing which he could not have meant
To prove the Christ was heaven sent!
Yet there they are, o genealogical sleuth:
Bathsheba, Tamar, Rahab, Ruth, recorded in the book of Truth.
Perhaps, if this was *meant* to be, it means God changes history
With folks who aren't celebrities, but people just like you and me.
Within your genealogy, what changes will yet come to be?
What names will people someday see, and what will be your legacy?

3 Tamar

December 3 Lust, Betrayal and Deception Prepare the Way for the Messiah

Tamar was the first woman mentioned in Matthew's genealogy, and has perhaps the most unusual story, from Genesis 38. (It would make an excellent mini-series for today's television audiences since it is full of mature content and contains allusions to violence and sexual abuse). She was a Canaanite woman married to Judah's son Er, who died prematurely. (Well, actually the Bible says the Lord ended his life because he was evil). She was left a childless widow, basically at the mercy of her in-laws.

In that culture, it was incredibly important to honor God by having offspring to carry on the family name. So, Judah instructed Er's brother Onan to fulfill his duty by impregnating Tamar. He had sex with her but stopped short of impregnating her. Apparently, God took this very seriously, because He ended Onan's life. These two brothers were not exactly shining examples of moral goodness, and poor Tamar was caught in the middle of all of it.

Judah had a young (remaining) son Shelah, but didn't want to risk him (since he'd already lost his two older sons), so he sent Tamar back to her home, hoping she'd forget all this and go away.

The young widow Tamar-- alone, traumatized, used, rejected by Judah and his sons, separated now from Yahweh's people, and mistreated in the eyes of the law—could have slunk home and into obscurity. But she apparently wanted God's blessing and favor so much that she'd do anything to get it.

So, she veiled herself, posed as a prostitute on the road where Judah would be traveling, and got Judah to take a break from his road trip and have sex with her. Because she was veiled, he did not recognize her, and she required him to leave his ring, his corded belt and his staff as payment. (I said it was an unusual story). Normally, for her to act as a prostitute, it would be punishable by death. But Tamar's motives were pure, and in this circumstance, she was acting to fulfill God's law and honor God's intent.

Upon being found pregnant, she revealed her actions to Judah: "As she was being brought out, she sent a message to her father-in-law. "I am pregnant by the man who owns these," she said. And she added, "See if you recognize whose seal and cord and staff these are." Judah recognized them and said, "She is more righteous than I, since I wouldn't give her to my son Shelah." And he did not sleep with her again. (Genesis 38:25-26 NIV)

Tamar was restored to honor, and her son Perez is listed among Jesus' forefathers. It's a bit of a long story to say this: by including women at all, Matthew has broken more than just traditional genealogical lines. He has served notice that the coming Messiah is not necessarily what the Elders expected. His lineage not only involved a woman, but a NON-HEBREW woman. It was not a sudden, pristine royal birth, but an incredibly complex series of events, woven into a human history replete with evil men and messy circumstances. God's preparation for the coming one was amazing in its details, and astounding in its intent. This Jesus, born in Bethlehem, did not have your "average" genealogy. But then, he was not your "average" guy.

The Ring, the Belt, and the Staff

This story in the Bible has me just a bit confused;
It seems to be about a girl who's sexually abused.
Tamar lost her husband, was rejected and alone,
And just decided she would solve this problem on her own.
She exercised her widow's right to bear a family son,
By fooling Judah into bed, and when the deed was done,
He paid the bill by giving her his ring, and belt, and staff—
When she conceived, I'm sure she had a brief, triumphant laugh!
There's cheating and betrayal, there is intrigue and there's lying;
Men are sneaking out with roadside hookers. Men are dying,
And this story's in the BIBLE! The Messiah's family tree!
The Bible says some stuff that I just didn't expect to see!
It speaks of lust and lying, and the type of stuff men do;
It's honest and it's real, and I believe it must be true;
I didn't see it all until I read it, through and through.
I wonder, when you read, what does the Bible say to YOU?

4 Rahab

December 4   Rahab the Harlot

"Then Joshua son of Nun secretly sent two spies from Shittim. "Go, look over the land," he said, "especially Jericho." So they went and entered the house of a prostitute named Rahab and stayed there. (Joshua 2:1 NIV)
[Rahab said] "Now then, please swear to me by the Lord that you will show kindness to my family, because I have shown kindness to you. Give me a sure sign that you will spare the lives of my father and mother, my brothers and sisters, and all who belong to them—and that you will save us from death." (Joshua 2:12-13 NIV)

Rahab of Jericho is another very unusual entry in Matthew's genealogy of Jesus. Not only is she a non-Hebrew woman, she is also a prostitute. By most cultural standards, she didn't exactly possess the desired pedigree a king would normally want to claim... And if you think about it, she wasn't just a prostitute, she was a traitor who sold out her own city. She harbored spies! She negotiated her freedom with an invading army! How on earth is she worthy of being mentioned in the Messiah's lineage? Why would Matthew include HER? (Surely if he wanted this genealogy to be palatable to Jewish readers, he could have left her out, or even made up someone who better fit into the Hebrew paradigm.)

This is one of those details that speaks to the authenticity of the Bible. Matthew could have left it out or written around it, but he brazenly tells us that one of Jesus' forebears was a lowly female who was an even lowlier prostitute who betrayed her city. Why did Rahab make this list?
Well first of all, she believed God. She had heard what was going on with the Israelites and believed it was true. This option was open to everyone in the city, by the way, but only Rahab took it. And second, she asked for redemption not only for her life, but for the lives of her entire family. What do you think would have happened to her if the king of Jericho had discovered her deception? She put herself at risk to save them all. She traded her past, she traded her citizenship, and she traded her future to the God of the Israelites.

What, Paul Harvey might ask, is the rest of Rahab's story? She was the mother of Boaz, and the great great grandmother of King David, arguably the greatest king in Israel's history. Pretty impressive for a lowly prostitute... How on earth did that happen? What was her secret of success, and what does it have to do with us??

If you look in Hebrews 11, among the great heroes of the faith, where the list includes Abraham, Joseph, Moses, you find this: "By faith the prostitute Rahab, because she welcomed the spies, was not killed with those who were disobedient." (Hebrews 11:31 NIV) Apparently EVERYBODY in Jericho had heard what God was doing, but no one else became obedient to Him because of it. Scripture infers that Jericho's citizens (Jerichonians?) were killed because they were disobedient. They had the same information that Rahab had. In Joshua 2:9-11, she tells the spies as much when she says, "All who live in this country are melting in fear because of you". But only Rahab had faith in God and acted upon it at great risk to herself. As a result, we got Boaz, Obed, and Jesse. We got King David (yeah, of "David and Goliath"). And oh yeah, we got the PSALMS. And the Messiah. Ask yourself: if God could do that much through a hooker in Jericho, what on earth could he do through YOU? Have some faith, and obey. Maybe someday they'll write a book about you!

Rahab's Choice

Jericho was a fortress strong, with walls as tall as they were long!
So, Joshua sent two men to seek and find if the defense was weak.
A Prostitute then took them in, a woman shamed and hurt by sin,
Who knew about this God they served. The city was a bit unnerved,
But Rahab risked her life to hide the spies she harbored there inside.
"Before you men complete your task, I have one thing that I must ask:
When Yahweh gives you victory, I ask that you remember me."
Thus Rahab's family was spared, since she believed and since she dared!
A lowly harlot came to be in Matthew's genealogy,
A prostitute who cheated death because she had obedient faith.
Her faith would indirectly bring to Israel her greatest king,
Descended from her as the one we came to know as Jesse's son.
So Rahab's risk—despite her qualms—resulted in the book of Psalms.
It's just the same with you and me. The Lord can alter history,
Perhaps because of what **you** do. In Rahab's life we know it's true:
What changes will you start by following God with all your heart?
What would your book say if you were following God TODAY?

5 Naomi and Ruth

December 5   Naomi and Ruth: a Love Story of Loyalty and Redemption

The third woman mentioned in Matthew's genealogy is Ruth, a young woman from Moab who married a man from Bethlehem. Moabites descended from Abraham's nephew Lot, so they were somewhat akin to Israel, although they worshipped other gods and fought with Saul, David and Solomon. The four Chapter book of the Bible bearing her name, which was set in the period of the Judges, tells how both her father-in-law and her husband died, and her mother-in-law (Naomi) gave her permission to return to her people and their gods.

Naomi reasoned that her own prospects for marriage were nonexistent (which certainly guaranteed her household a life of poverty), and so she told her daughter-in-law that she should go back to her own people, find herself a husband, and make a new life. Ruth's statement to her mother-in-law Naomi is one of the most oft-quoted Old Testament statements about love and loyalty: "And Ruth said, Entreat me not to leave thee, or to return from following after thee: for whither thou goest I will go, and where thou lodgest, I will lodge; thy people shall be my people, and thy God my God: where thou diest, I will die, and there will I be buried. The Lord do so to me, and more also, if ought but death part thee and me." (Ruth 1:16-17, NKJV) Rather than returning to her own people, Ruth expressed such love for Naomi that she was willing to stay by her side even though they faced hardship and a very questionable future.

Ruth's story takes an amazing turn when, while gathering leftover grain, following the reapers, she is noticed by Boaz, the owner of the field. Boaz was a kinsman of Naomi's deceased husband, and custom allowed destitute relatives to gather leftover scraps of the harvest in order to survive. Naomi seems to know something of Boaz, and she may have had more than a little bit of a scheme going on by getting Ruth into Boaz' field. By the same token, Boaz is aware of Ruth's loyalty to Naomi, and very favorably impressed not only by this familial loyalty but by Ruth herself.

This love story has a beautiful ending, as Ruth and Naomi are rescued from poverty when Boaz, acting in his role as a kinsman redeemer, secures the right to marry Ruth and start a family. Their son Obed was David's grandfather. A couple of things: Naomi's somewhat transparent scheming was not subverted or rejected by God. I think that discovering God's will does not always require us to sit passively by while we wait for Him to act, and I think He even honors those who pursue His favor with passion. Second, the role of kinsman redeemer was apparently common knowledge to Naomi, Boaz, and the other people in their village. The women even sing about Naomi's good fortune in having a kinsman in 4:14. We are going to take a deeper look at Boaz and his response as Ruth's (and Naomi's) redeemer tomorrow, but suffice it to say that this love story built on humility, loyalty, perseverance (and perhaps Naomi's feminine wiles) is not put in Christ's lineage by accident.

This series of events points to David—who obviously got some of his passion and love from his grandmother—and to Jesus the Messiah, who would both preach about and be characterized by these qualities. The inclusion of a Moabite woman points to the coming Messiah's inclusion of people outside of Israel. The story of her being rescued by a kinsman redeemer is a flashing neon sign announcing that the Messiah's work will redeem the disadvantaged, the dispossessed, the downcast... If you've ever been in one of those categories, or are now, take heart: the Redeemer has come, and he wants to rescue you.

Entreat Me Not to Leave Thee

Naomi's life was stripped of joys:
Her husband died, and then her boys;
She faced a future full of grief without much prospect of relief...
She told her daughters-in-law to leave
And build their lives; Yes, she would grieve,
But they should go and carry on while she remained behind, alone.
And one of them took the open door;
It just made sense. They'd be so poor,
And living would be a daily grind: but one of them remained behind.
Naomi had told the girls the truth, so now she really questioned Ruth:
She said she shouldn't waste her youth
By living on a widow's mite. It wasn't good. It wasn't right.
But Ruth could only shake her head.
She hugged Naomi. Then she said:
"Please do not entreat me to forsake or ever leave Thee.
I'll stay with you forever, though the valley be so low;
Though this life may break you, this my love will not forsake you.
I will love Thy God, and there is one thing you should know...
So listen to what I have to say: Whither thou stayest, I will stay,
And from this moment, come what may, whither thou goest, I will go."

6 Boaz

December 6   The Kinsman Redeemer

Ruth's declaration of love and loyalty didn't keep Naomi from feeling despair at first. She told her friends that they should change her name to Mara (bitter), "because the almighty has made my life very bitter..." They returned to Bethlehem in time for the harvest, and Ruth went to work as a peasant in the fields of a man named Boaz. When Ruth told Naomi that she had met Boaz, and that he had spoken kindly to her, Naomi said, "The Lord bless him! He has not stopped showing his kindness to the living and the dead." She added, "That man is our close relative; he is one of our kinsman-redeemers." (Ruth 2:20, NIV)

Old Testament law stipulated that the nearest kinsman would offer to marry a brother's widow and carry on his name, to offer redemption to relatives sold into slavery, and to avenge the killing of a relative. You think there is drama in YOUR family? Imagine what types of unusual human interaction might have taken place under some of those circumstances! A brother-in-law might think his brother's widow is too ugly to marry. Or, like Onan with Tamar, he might use her without fulfilling his obligation. Or an opportunistic redeemer might take advantage of those too helpless to avoid him (think: Evil Stepmother in Cinderella)

Even though there were risks involved in this type of process, this unusual avenue to redemption had plenty of upside. A good kinsman-redeemer offered hope to the hopeless, offered help to the helpless, and provided a chance to live a life changed by redemption. A kinsman-redeemer bought you back out of slavery or hopelessness and adopted you into his family. (Hmmm, just like the Messiah was going to do...)

In this case, Boaz is a kind, godly man who respects Ruth and protects her reputation even when she follows Naomi's advice: she makes herself vulnerable by crawling into bed with the sleeping Boaz and warming his feet (which could have been interpreted as an act of service OR the actions of a loose woman). Not only does he treat her with respect but he goes on to observe all the requirements of the law with scrupulous honesty and transparency to the elders in the village, and he makes Ruth his wife in front of God and everybody.

The Elders were prophetic when they said, "Through the offspring the Lord gives you by this young woman, may your family be like that of Perez, whom Tamar bore to Judah." (Ruth 4:12) Sure enough, Ruth and Boaz' son Obed was King David's grandfather. Still very close to her mother-in-law, Ruth allowed Naomi to act as his nurse, giving her a family again. So what did the women of the village say to Naomi about Ruth? Nothing but the highest praise: "Your daughter-in-law, who loves you... is better to you than seven sons." These two widows went from bitter circumstances to the comforting house of their kinsman-redeemer. Boaz's kindness redeemed both Ruth and Naomi, and changed their lives forever. Ours, too, by the way...

The Widow's Redeemer Who Changed the World

A widow who was destitute was working in the field
Picking up the scraps after the workers took the yield.
The owner saw her beauty and integrity revealed,
And watched her do her job with admiration unconcealed.

He had to find out who she was as soon as he had seen her;
Some owners might abuse her, or they might just treat her meaner,
But he found out that he was nearest kinsman and redeemer;
And he decided then that he would pay for and redeem her.

He spoke then with the village elders, and he made it known
That he would take this widow and reclaim her as his own.
He also said Naomi wouldn't have to be alone,
Since he was taking both of them to live within his home.

Ruth and Boaz raised a son, and Obed was his name.
Obed had a boy named Jesse; then some Grandsons came.
From them, David killed Goliath, rose to wealth and fame,
And through his life, the world we know has never been the same!
You may not be famous, but I know this is the truth:
The Lord may change the world through YOU,
 Just like He did with Ruth.

7 The Woman Who Was Not Named

December 7   Bathsheba proves that Grace is Not A Merit System

The fourth woman named in Matthew's genealogy isn't really ever named outright, but we know who she is. He says, "David was the father of Solomon, whose mother had been Uriah's wife." (Matt 1:6) He never gives her name directly, but we can surely connect the dots back to King David's greatest personal failure...

Out of all the royal wives in Israel's history, Bathsheba was always connected to Israel's greatest king, and to the king's greatest sin—and yet it was she who was chosen to carry the line of the Messiah. Perhaps her name was so tarnished that Matthew couldn't bring himself to say it. Perhaps, unlike a Ruth or a Rahab, she was unworthy somehow. (This is another one of those accurate details that a more polished narrative would have glossed over somehow. Unlike in today's politics, the Bible keeps telling the truth when a lie would work so much better...)

But the surprising thing is this: David had other sons by other wives, and yet Bathsheba's son Solomon bore the royal lineage. Why did God choose her and him? Two things: first, Bathsheba was more than just a pretty face. She was apparently a pretty shrewd player in palace politics. When Adonijah (not her son) proclaimed himself to be king, she risked her own life to present her case to the aged and infirm King David: "Bathsheba bowed down, prostrating herself before the king. "What is it you want?" the king asked. She said to him, "My lord, you yourself swore to me your servant by the Lord your God: 'Solomon your son shall be king after me, and he will sit on my throne.' But now Adonijah has become king, and you, my lord the king, do not know about it." (1 Kings 1:16-18 NIV)

She brought in Nathan the prophet as an ally, and David confirmed his oath to make Solomon King. Without her brazen resolve, who knows if Solomon would have gained the throne? Or lived another day? In the midst of dangerous and volatile circumstances, she asked the king to keep his promises. Perhaps that is something all of us should do...

Second, I am kinda glad that someone who was connected to such terrible and far-reaching mistakes (David and Bathsheba aren't the only ones in the genealogy who qualify, by the way) still made this list. It's not a merit system. The Messiah does not judge you by your mistakes. If you have been less than perfect, if you have committed egregious errors, and even if your mistakes have had gut-wrenching and far-reaching consequences, take heart. Jesus understands that stuff because it's all over the place in his family tree. And he said this: "For I have not come to call the righteous, but sinners." (Matthew 9:13 NIV)

That's Good Christmas news for Bathsheba and David. Good news for Solomon. And very good news for us.

David, Bathsheba and Grace

A man of passion, power and might,
The jaded king would find the sight
Of a naked beauty he did not know
An utterly enticing show...

So, David called Bathsheba in;
Temptation led to secret sin:
Clandestine meetings, broken trust
And finally, to murderous lust!

And yet these sins, and this disgrace
Did not prevent unfailing Grace,
Or let this evil undermine
The course of the Messiah's line...

If you look through it, you can see
In Matthew's genealogy
Imperfect folks like you and me.
From sinners, God made history!

From folks who knew of sin and shame,
The heavenly Messiah came!
Perfection, this Bathsheba missed:
But by God's Grace, she made this list.
Though Matthew doesn't say her name,
The world through her would never be the same.

8 Mary

December 8   It Seems Obvious, So why Doesn't Everybody Do it?

The last woman mentioned in Matthew's genealogy is the most obvious one: "and Mary was the mother of Jesus who is called the Messiah." (Matthew 1:16, NIV). Mary lived a remarkable life, and was certainly a remarkable young woman. With all of the legend and adulation that has grown up around her, all of the Da Vinci code supposition and mystery, she is surely the most revered woman in history.

From our vantage point, there is not all that much in the Bible to go on in terms of getting to know her, but she seems to be a fairly normal, if somewhat more devout girl of her times. She was chosen for a mission that rearranged her life in the most uncomfortable ways possible—pregnant and possibly disgraced on the cusp of her nuptials, targeted by gossips and disapproving eyes, forced to go live with her cousin in the hill country...

Not everything was easy and glorious for Mary. Even years later, the Pharisees, arguing with Jesus about his paternity, sneered, "WE are not illegitimate children!" (John 8:41), so Mary's predicament in being pregnant outside of marriage was obviously public knowledge, and the story followed Jesus into adulthood.

It may be hard to see from this side of history, on this side of the veneration and adulation of Mary, but at one time she was a simple village girl from Nazareth who was visited by a messenger who had a word from God. She was fearful and a bit skeptical (you can read about it in Luke 1), but after weighing her options and resolving her questions, said to Gabriel: "I am the Lord's servant. May your word to me be fulfilled." It strikes me that this answer probably contains pretty good clues about attitude for all of us when life throws us a curve ball.

First, remember who God is and who we are. Mary calls herself "the Lord's servant", meaning that when she calls God, "Lord", she means it. He is above her, and she is willing and ready to put him first, even in some crazy circumstances. I'd see this as a good attitude for us to have when life gives us unexpected difficulties. It probably helped Mary to have an angel deliver God's Word, but we aren't off the hook on that one, since we have the Word at our disposal 24/7. We can whine, "God didn't give me a message!"—but maybe it's been available to us all along and we just haven't read it. Has God sent you a messenger lately? Are you listening?

Second, she is obedient to God. No protest, no argument. A puzzled question about logistics, but that's it. "May your word to me be fulfilled." I'd suggest that if all of us took TODAY, and prayed this little prayer—"May your Word to me be fulfilled"—(and meant it), we'd have a different outlook, and a different kind of day. And if we did it EVERY day, we'd have a different kind of life. Mary certainly did: not by magic, or even by angelic proclamation, but by obedience and faith. Those are the tools. Here is your day.

Be It to Me According to Thy Word: the YES that Changed Everything

Christmas is a happy time, so full of joy and giving!
It is a time of hope, reminding us that life's worth living!
We all enjoy the lovely sights of mistletoe and Christmas lights,
And gathering with family to eat our Christmas-time delights.
We watch our favorite Christmas movie features on TV,
And marvel at the stack of presents underneath the tree!
But tell me, as you think of Christmas (maybe with some snow!),
And shop for presents dodging Christmas traffic as you go,
Would there be a Santa, would there be some mistletoe?
What would our world be like today if Mary had just said, "No"?
If Mary said no, this world would be a totally different place,
Without our Christmas giving, and with far less hope and grace.
If she said no, our world would hold more shame, and more disgrace.
Well... what if YOU said No to God? What difference would there be?
What grace and hope would future generations fail to see?
What priceless gifts would languish under history's Christmas tree?
Mary changed the world by saying "Yes" to God's request;
But what if God called all of us, and ALL of us said yes?
You know how God used Mary's yes, I guess you know the rest...

9 The Messenger
December 9   Believing in an Unbelievable Message

There is much to learn from Mary's response to God's messenger. (And by the way, the Greek word for angel is αγγελος, or messenger—simply put, a courier who brings a message, or a word from someone else). In Mary's case, she was clearly being given direction from God, and I guess it's conceivable that she could have fought against it or rebelled against such a life-changing commission; but she didn't.

Perhaps YOU have heard a message from God yourself lately, or even read one on your own...How did you react to it? After she heard what Gabriel had to say, she said, "May your word to me be fulfilled."

His word was this: "You will conceive and give birth to a son, and you are to call him Jesus. He will be great and will be called the Son of the Most High. The Lord God will give him the throne of his father David, and He will reign over Jacob's descendants forever; his kingdom will never end." (Luke 1:31-33, NIV)

Basically, Gabriel brought a word from God, quoting the word of God about the Word of God, and Mary (and Joseph as well) had absolute faith in the message. She affirmed it verbally, and then she lived it obediently. The first-born son was not going to be Bar-Joseph according to custom, but was to be given a name indicative of who he was. Jesus is a shortened form of Joshua, derived from Jehoshuah, which in the Hebrew means "Jehovah is salvation." Gabriel points to Isaiah 9:6-7, which says "unto us a son is born", and refers to God's promise of an eternal throne to David's line in 2 Samuel 7:12-14.

As Mary listened to his message, she undoubtedly found comfort in the fact that this birth had been foretold...There are in fact over FOUR HUNDRED references in the Old Testament that are prophecies connected to Jesus' birth, life and death. (You can Google that!) They are like hundreds of threads woven in to the Old Testament out of all space and time to create a tapestry of hope, pointing towards Jesus of Nazareth. The authors (Moses, David, Isaiah, Jeremiah, Daniel, Micah, Zechariah) wrote independently and without any way of knowing the timing, the person, or the outcome of their books, but their words connected the dots between God's covenant people and the promised Redeemer.

Let's say you're skeptical about that, or just don't think all four hundred plus prophecies really apply... Even if some of them are a bit of a stretch, or if some of them are hard to connect—let's say we throw out *half* of them—wouldn't you think that someone whose birth was foretold by a couple of hundred predictions from centuries before would justify some serious thought?

Those writers certainly didn't know who Jesus was going to be, or when he would be born, but there were too many uncannily accurate prophecies about Jesus' arrival to easily dismiss. From the Tribe of Judah. (Micah 5:2) From Jesse's family (Isaiah 11:1) and David's line (Jeremiah 23:5-6). Announced by a messenger (Isaiah 40:3; Malachi 3:1). Preceded by a star (Numbers 24:17). Born of a Virgin (Isaiah 7:14). Born in Bethlehem (Micah 5:2). Called Immanuel (God with us) (Isaiah 7:14). Weeping in Ramah (Jeremiah 31:15). Flight to Egypt (Hosea 11:1). He would be worshipped and presented gifts by kings (Psalm 72:10).

Consider this: there is NO other historical figure (including Mohammed and Buddha) whose coming was foretold in such volume and detail, or so far in advance. **No One**. Since the angel was pretty specific in mentioning these OT quotes in his message to Mary, they at least bear some consideration relative to who Jesus was.

Ok, so why am I talking about the messenger, and the message to Mary? Because when Gabriel made his announcement to her, it was also a message to **everyone** who would come after. It was a message to me. It was a message to **you as well**. It seems we all have the same choice before us that Mary had: we can believe the word of the messenger, and then live differently because of it; or we can dismiss it, and go on as if nothing had happened. I think something happened. If Gabriel's word was fulfilled, as Mary hoped and affirmed, then it's worth looking into.

The Messenger and the Choice

What Gabriel said to Mary must have scared her through and through;
But as unbelievable as it seemed, she did what she had to do.
Well, what if Gabriel's message **then** was also meant for YOU?
What about the prophecy and things that men foreknew?
Would it change your life if you believed that it was true?
Could you be obedient if you believed it, too?

10 John's Testimony
December 10   Thy Word Made Flesh

Yesterday we said that Mary heard a word from God, quoting the word of God about the Word of God... John said it this way: "In the beginning was the Word, and the Word was with God, and the Word was God. He was with God in the beginning. Through him all things were made; without him nothing was made that has been made. In him was life, and that life was the light of all mankind. The light shines in the darkness, and the darkness has not overcome it... The Word became flesh and made his dwelling among us. We have seen his glory, the glory of the one and only Son, who came from the Father, full of grace and truth." (John 1:1-5, 14 NIV)

When Mary said, "Be it unto me according to thy word", John's amazing prologue characterizing Jesus as the Word, or the logos, had not yet been written. In this opening paragraph to his gospel, John says that the Word was eternally preexistent, was with God and indeed was God. This Word was the Creator and the source of all life and illumination in the cosmos. John says that the Word came and dwelt among men, who could see its glory.

The concept of men receiving the word of the Lord was fairly common in the OT. God's Spirit moved among men and imparted His words to the prophets, gave instruction, and prophesied about things to come. God's word appeared or was given to men for a task or a season, but it was not an abiding presence on the earth. For instance, 1 Samuel 3:1 says that "the word of the Lord was scarce in those days". At other times men like Abraham (Genesis 15:1, "The word of the Lord came to Abram in a vision") and Moses, who was "commanded by the word of the Lord" (Numbers 3:16, 51) encountered God's word in life changing ways. The prophets were moved to speak because of it. "The word of the Lord came to Elijah" (1 Kings 18:1) and Zephaniah 1:1 attributes his prophecy to the word of the Lord.

There are well over 200 references to the word of God in the Old Testament, so John's reference to the Word was not unique in Jewish Scripture; but the idea that the Word could become an actual person and dwell among men was entirely foreign to the Hebrew mind and heritage. By introducing Christ as the Word, John makes some astounding claims about a man who he knew well-- someone he hung out with, traveled with, and observed at close range for at least three years. Think about those whom you know, the folks you joke with or party with; chances are you know them far too well to equate them with God, or to ever actually call them God... Yet John did exactly that with Jesus. Why do you think he did that? Answer THAT question, and I bet you'll answer a whole bunch of other ones...

The Writer

Youngest disciple, did you know where all the twists and turns would go,
And did you have a line of sight to what would come from what you'd write?
Jesus' loved one, did you think, when struggling with your quill and ink,
That History hung on every word you wrote of what you'd seen and heard?
Out to a thoughtless, careless world, your personal account was hurled:
The words of a crazy, exiled Jew, who claimed that what he'd seen was true!
Could you have known? Could you have seen
The phrasing there, in three sixteen,
And you could somehow sense, or see, down corridors of History,
That someday it would come to me, affecting what **my** life would be?
Some might say you were misled, or somehow addled in your head,
And some with proud disdain despise your testament, and call it lies...
But some say that you have a friend whose kingdom's come, and will not end,
Who showed you love as meant to be, by being who He was sent to be!
Jesus' Beloved, Apostle John, your words live now, and will live on
For us, from what you saw and heard, and captured in your timeless word:
For all the world—for everyone—God gave his only precious son,
That all who seek Him, and believe, will each eternal life receive.
The perfect love that fell on Thee has fallen, too, on me...

11 The Living Word

December 11   The Word was God

"In the beginning was the Word, and the Word was with God, and the Word was God." (John 1:1 NIV) Where Matthew and Luke provide historical and genealogical context for Jesus' arrival, John's gospel explores the theological implications...

He starts his gospel by describing the Word in cosmic terms that transcend time and space, terms that offer no equivocation or apology. The idea of the logos, or true word, had been floating around philosophical circles for several centuries. Heraclitus used the term as a principle for order and knowledge as early as 500 BC. Sophists like Aristotle used it to describe discourse, and Stoics believed it was "the divine animating principle pervading the universe". Philo (20 BC-AD 50) was a Hellenistic Jewish philosopher and contemporary of John's who adopted it into Jewish philosophy.

Brought into the English language, all of these uses and definitions fail to capture or describe the full breadth of meaning behind logos, which conveyed generative force and dynamic thought to first century users. John takes this word, however and gives it a unique application that changed and challenged everything. John's introduction of this concept creates the basis for a radical and revolutionary change in all religious and spiritual thought up to that time.

John says in 1:14 that "the Word was made flesh, and dwelt among us..." This connects Jesus to John's opening sentence, "In the beginning was the Word, and the Word was with God and the Word was God." This is one of the most insightful and important sentences ever written. It provides cohesion and context for the Christ's place in the Bible, and presents Jesus as the incarnate word who connects the Old Testament with the New. Consider these connections: The Pentateuch opens with, "in the beginning, GOD..." So does John. "God created". So did the Word. "God said..."

The Word created. (As an aside, when it comes to creation, I find it fascinating that adherents of a Big Bang theory, who believe passionately in following scientific method, can leap by assumption to a very complex set of conditions that are based on preexisting elements which were NOT recorded or observable. They contend that things happened randomly but exactly in a certain way at the beginning of all things—and they can hold this position in face of incredibly long odds in terms of actual probability—and then they can turn around and be critical of a hypothesis that rationally assumes a preexistent God, with creation and origin coming from the one who already existed in the beginning, and who expressed himself creatively. That kind of assumptive science is faith of a sort, at best; but it is scientific hypocrisy, at worst...)

John talks about the Word who was with God and who WAS God. The Greek syntax where John says "the Word was God" is such that the two parts are identical and interchangeable: the Word = God, and God = the Word. There is no ambiguity about Jesus' identity in either this statement or in the other Gospels... Matthew connects Jesus' birth to the Messiah who had long been foretold. Luke connects Jesus to mankind by tracing his genealogy back to Adam... and John? Well, he connects Jesus **to God**. If those connections are correct, then Jesus wasn't just a Jewish prophet, and he wasn't just a good man: he was God. That's not just a good word, it is THE Word. Always has been. Always will be.

The Word

The universe was not a bang or something that just occurred,
But cosmic energy released within the spoken word.
"In the beginning was The Word." John said this long before
Eternity past created what the future holds, and more...
Eons can be relative, and time may seem to plod,
But the Word transcended time and space because the Word was God.
That Word, John said, became a man, and we beheld his glory,
His execution of the plan to tell redemption's story.
Of all the things you've read and out of everything you've heard,
Consider this: The Word was God. And Jesus was the Word.

12 The Son of Man
December 12   The Word was Man

John's insights about the "Word made flesh" (about Jesus) in his Gospel's introduction are pretty compelling. Not only does he say that Jesus was God, and was preexistent from the beginning, he says "Through him all things were made; without him nothing was made that has been made." (John 1:3 NIV) Since Jesus was not just a man, John enlarges upon what that means. As the Word, Jesus was the creative part of God's personality. "God SAID, Let there be light, and there was light." God spoke the universe into existence. Jesus was literally the Word who created this universe, the heavens, and this world...

This is an area that I think we humans might have a hard time grasping in all of its implications, both spiritually and emotionally. As the preexistent creative personality of God, Jesus spoke, energized and framed the cosmos into existence. Colossians 1:17 says "He is before all things, and in him all things hold together." Jesus, the word incarnate, came to earth as a man and lived upon the planet he had made. The earth and all that had sprung from it were his creation, the expression of his creative power and intent.

How do you think he sometimes felt, walking upon the very earth he had spoken into existence? Sitting under a tree to find protection from the sun he had made? Looking up and identifying the stars at night? Drinking cold water after a dusty walk? I'd bet that the strongest maternal instinct would pale in comparison to the intimacy Jesus felt with his creation...

And on the other side of that equation, do you think that fallen man's mistreatment of it, and of each other, ever broke his heart? As he saw the selfishness, the cruelty, the tragedy in his world, do you think he ever thought, this is not what I intended? That I will do whatever it takes to fix this? (Hmmm, does he ever say that just looking into **your** heart?)

The Word made flesh—which is the Advent, which is Christmas—means that he came to earth and literally became part of his own creation to do something about it regardless of the immeasurable cost. He often referred to himself as "the Son of Man", claiming a title in Ezekiel 33:22; he not only related to the world as His creation, but he fully embraced his humanity, even though He was not of this world. He was a man, yes, but a man who lived with heavenly standards in order to show us our heavenly potential. We should live, then, as he intended. Perhaps it would help if we saw the world around us through His eyes, if we appreciated it with His love... It might help us to look beyond the commercial Capitalist Christmas or the selfish shopper who stole my parking space. It might help us disengage from the whirlwind of activities to some private reflection about Christ—the FIRST syllable of Christmas...

This Christmas season, put on your Holiday glasses of grace and see the world the way its Creator saw it, the way he intended it to be. And while you're at it, look at yourself the same way, with more than a mother's matchless love. If you think Jesus loved his creation, then imagine how he feels about YOU. See? There really are good tidings of great joy at Christmas!

The Word Made Flesh

Of all the things that men have said,
The one that makes you scratch your head
Is John's assertion that the Cosmic plan
Involves Almighty God becoming man.
How ludicrous that claim must be!
Why, any fool could clearly see
That God's incredible, matchless worth
Would never limit itself to earth!
But if He did... what things would He must have felt!
What air he breathed! And when he stooped and knelt
To touch the grass, to break an earthen clod:
What did he think-- the Word, Creator, God?
Surely he enjoyed what he had made--
A cold refreshing drink beneath the shade,
Laughter where the children ran and played;
The sunsets, with His handiwork displayed...
Surely he loved creation more than most;
He knew far better all that had been lost:
Knew its value, and He knew the cost.
He knew the covenants, knew they'd not been kept;
He stood above Jerusalem, and wept.
And then this God-- this Galilean Jew
Gave up his life to rescue me. And you.
I wonder-- the Bible never makes this clear--
Did He miss heaven more when he came down here,
Or after all He'd said, and seen, and done,
Did He miss us as much when He went home?

13 Christmas Life, Christmas Light

December 13   In Him was Life; and that Life was the Light of Men

Of this baby born in Bethlehem, John said, "In him was life, and that life was the light of men. The light shines in the darkness, but the darkness has not understood it." (John 1:4-5, NIV) It is really easy to not understand Jesus... and one of the easiest ways to do that is to assume you already know, and to avoid really looking at him.

People often look at small snapshots of Jesus without ever watching the whole movie. Or they assume that Jesus must be like people who say they know him, and the spectrum of behavior from folks who say they follow Jesus can be both incredibly varied and incredibly misleading. They range from misguided religious nuts to sincere believers who make mistakes, still live in the flesh, and yes, still commit sins...

It's very easy, if you are skeptical, to look at the Church—the imperfect, stumbling, bumbling followers of Christ and decide Jesus is not for you. Or it's easy to avoid looking at him closely. So many people say, "Yeah, I know about Jesus, I know about his teachings", when all they have done is given a cursory glance at what he said, or listened to a secondhand account (yeah, like this one) of what he said.

But I would say that to anyone who encounters the Jesus of the Bible, the rabbi who gave the Sermon on the Mount, the teacher who confounded the Pharisees, or the healer who healed, the same man whose birthday we celebrate every year at Christmas, John's description of the Word is accurate and applicable. After 3 years of walking daily with Jesus, of watching him heal and listening to him teach, and after having meals and walking along the road and going to parties with him, he understood who Jesus was, and he captured it perfectly here in his introduction: "In him was life."

To Jairus' daughter in Luke 8, Jesus was life; To Lazarus in John 11, Jesus was life; to the thief on the cross beside him in Luke 23, Jesus was life. To Stephen in Acts 7, even as he fell beneath the stones, Jesus was life. Saul of Tarsus, better known as the Apostle Paul, said, "For me to live is Christ, and to die is gain." (Philippians 1:21) To me, in the 20th century as an insecure teenager, Jesus was life.

Question: have you REALLY investigated Jesus of Nazareth? Do you know what he taught, have you truly looked at what he was about? John says that "in him was life, and that life was the light of men." I would suggest that there is indeed darkness in this world, and that the darkness not only doesn't understand Jesus, it doesn't want anyone else to understand him either. To those who understand Jesus and discover life in the Word, John promises illumination in the darkness. He promises the ability to see new things, to grow, to stretch outward and upward to life-giving rays of hope! I hope you investigate. I hope you understand. You know who said, "I am come that they might have life, and have it more abundantly"? Yep. But don't take MY word for it.

The Life of Heaven. The Light of Men

John walked with Jesus every day. He talked with him along the way;
He heard what Jesus had to say.
He ate with him. He watched him pray.
He saw the things that no one sees,
saw him confound the Pharisees!
He heard him preach and saw him heal,
and decided Jesus was for real.
Then, finally, he wrote a book. It's short. Go read it, take a look-
A book I heartily commend, John's own account of his best friend:
He wrote this down, and it's worth saying again:
"In Him was life. He was the Light of Men."

14 How Much Light Do You Need?

December 14   The Light that Helps You See

John refers to the Word as "the true light that gives light to every man". (John 1:9, NIV) I used to think this couldn't be true, since not every man may have had a chance to see or hear about Jesus (such as all who came before, or were raised in darkest Africa or China, where Jesus was not a household name...) But if he was the Word, the creative expression of God's personality, (John 1:3, "without him nothing was made that has been made) then it means every man is exposed to some revelation about God through the order and design of the universe, which reflect the creative nature and character of God. As Abraham Lincoln said, "I can see how it might be possible for a man to look down upon the earth and be an atheist, but I cannot conceive how a man could look up into the heavens and say there is no God."

We may not see Jesus directly, but because He is the Word who created all things, we see evidence of Him all around us, as well as above and beyond us. ("The heavens declare the glory of God, and the firmament shows his handiwork." Psalms 19:1) The thing is, God has given us evidence instead of proof so that we have a choice about faith. If I could PROVE God's existence to you, then you would HAVE to accept it, and faith would play no part in discovering who God is. The creation tells us much about God, but He has not directly revealed himself for good reason.

People who say to God, "Show me who you are and I'll accept it" are testing the God of the universe and telling Him to come to them on their own terms... CS Lewis points out that people who want God to appear before them may be asking the wrong question. "But I wonder whether people who ask God to interfere openly and directly in our world quite realize what it will be like when He does. When that happens, it is the end of the world. When the author walks on the stage the play is over... That will not be the time for choosing; it will be the time when we discover which side we really have chosen, whether we realized it before or not" (p. 65, Mere Christianity).

In our daily exposure to creative design, we encounter the Word of God. It is interesting to compare the teachings of Christ to the structure of the universe, and to see the intimate details wrought into galaxies and microbes, to realize just how astoundingly right John was. Jesus taught about agriculture, the Kingdom of Heaven, and about seeing the Father. There is beauty in the creator's handiwork that can only be discovered in the light of the Word. There is light coming to us from the vast reaches of space, from stars whose network of gravitational power holds us in exactly the right place in our solar system so that we can exist. There is light from our own sun, which keeps us from freezing, activates photosynthesis in plants, provides us with vitamins, and which makes it possible for us here on earth to experience life and growth. There is order in the way things operate, whether you look as far out into the heavens as you can, or as deeply into the microscope as it is possible to look. Every created thing reflects principles of order and design. God's handiwork displays infinite scale that is both massive and microscopic; there is relationship, there are consequences, there is harmony and truth. Go out to the country on a clear night and gaze into the stars, past the constellations and out into space. Think about the fact that some of the light your eyes can see has traveled thousands of light-years across space, and originated before the pyramids. See if your soul isn't stirred a bit, if you don't find yourself a little bit in awe of the Creator... Compare what you feel to what you know about the Word of God. It just may be that you are receiving more light out there than you ever realized before.

The Light of Men

John declared that the Word was light, that somewhere in God's plan
There is a revelation that has come to every man.
The skeptic calls this false, of course,
And says you cannot prove the source;
He hopes he will not have remorse,
But believes in a kind of cosmic force...
This kind of independent thinking prospers and persists
Since God will not force anyone to know that He exists.
He offers every man--not proof-- which would be undeniable;
But evidence, so that man's faith would not be unreliable.
It may seem right to look around, and ask God for a sign;
But if there's light when you look up, perhaps there is design...

15 Are You *Too* Familiar With Christmas?
December 15   Blinded by the Light?

"The true light that gives light to everyone was coming into the world. He was in the world, and though the world was made through him, the world did not recognize him. He came to that which was his own, but his own did not receive him." (John 1:9-11 NIV) In these verses, John refers to Jesus as the light of the world, and points out that not only was he unrecognized by the world at large, but he was not even received by his own people. How did that happen?

Paul says in 2 Corinthians 4:4 that there is an obvious reason why men fail to see: "The god of this age has blinded the minds of unbelievers, so that they cannot see the light of the gospel that displays the glory of Christ, who is the image of God." It is hard to see without light. I think I still have a scar on my shin from the time I hit the corner of a coffee table trying to traverse an unfamiliar hotel room in the dark. When you can't see, it can be painful.

So here's a simple intellectual principle from John 1: LIGHT HELPS YOU SEE. What is in your life that provides light for you? And what is it that shrouds you in darkness? What lifts you up, inspires you, and points your thinking towards discovery and truth? And what does the opposite of that? It's no accident that most violent crimes or despicable deeds are committed between midnight and four AM (although statistically many property crimes happen during the day, so be careful out there). John 3:19 reminds us that "Men loved darkness rather than light, because their deeds were evil."

Here in his introduction, John says the Word was the light of men, but that it wasn't recognized by the world. That's not too surprising, considering the Word did not share the world's values or agenda. The world is a pretty self-absorbed, self-centered place. (Been shopping or driving lately?) The Bible says that Satan holds sway over the earth, so really we should not be too surprised when we find selfishness or deceit all around us, whether in our politics or in our culture. Heck, we even find those things WITHIN us from time to time. Consider this: being involved in sinful selfishness has never really been a great way to find God... When you are focusing all your attention on worldly things, it's pretty hard to see the things of the Spirit, so it's hard to argue with John's statement about the world not recognizing the light. Maybe it's a little more surprising that Jesus' own people (chosen by God) did not receive him. They were a people who sacrificed for sin, read the prophets and prayed the Shema daily. They were taught to love God with all their heart and to keep the law, but when Jesus arrived they didn't receive him much more than the world did. Maybe they were caught up in their own agenda, or were closer to the world than they were to their roots. Or maybe they were TOO religious, and saw God as a legal system instead of a person. It's very easy to worship religion instead of God.

Two quick things: there is lots of stuff in this world that will keep you from seeing Jesus. Don't miss what he did; don't miss what he said. Second, we all sometimes assume that proximity or connection to something is enough. "I live in a Christian nation." "I read about Jesus in vacation Bible school." "I go to church." "I know the Golden Rule". Don't let familiarity keep you from seeing Jesus. His own people missed him. Just because you know SOME thing about him, don't assume you know HIM.

Familiarity Breeds Contempt

There are so many ways that you can miss the Gospel truth:
Assume, ignore, avoid-- or chase the foolishness of youth.
Sometimes what you think you know can lead you far astray,
While sometimes you don't see because there's something in the way.
Looking at the forest, it's the tree that no one sees,
Unless, of course you cannot see the forest for the trees...
You may have heard the saying, "familiarity breeds contempt";
Be careful, then, what you assume, for you are not exempt.
Lies can shackle judgment, but it is the truth that frees us;
So why not take a deeper look at the guy who said that: Jesus.

16 Christmas With the Royal Family

December 16   What Would It Be Like to Be in a Royal Family?

Christmas is certainly the story of a King, and it is something that adds to its mystique and magnitude, even more so when you consider this verse in John's prologue: "Yet to all who did receive him, to those who believed in his name, he gave the right to become children of God— children born not of natural descent, nor of human decision or a husband's will, but born of God." (John 1:12-13 NIV)

It would be pretty great to be part of a Royal Family. Many little girls dream of being a princess, and the Disney Princess industry is actually pretty astounding in the breadth of its offerings. There are shoes and dresses and tiaras and play sets and dolls and castles and jewelry and accessories, and oh so much more! Have you ever imagined being Royalty? To live in opulence, to have servants, to be part of the royal family? It's not something you can normally choose, it's something you have to be born into, or marry into if you are fortunate enough. Maybe we could apply for a job as a servant in the palace, but that's the only way we would ever walk the Royal halls...

In our world the average person has a much better chance of winning the lottery than of becoming part of a Royal family; yet John's amazing introduction suggests that it is an option open to everyone. When he presents the Word made flesh, he ties the Bethlehem manger directly to the heavenly palace. This baby who was born in an obscure place and away from the mainstream of worldly power had the authority to confer citizenship in a new kingdom.

But wait, there's more! He also brought every one of us the right to become children of God. As opposed to human convention, religious systems or earthly royalty, this adoption into God's family did not depend on money or pedigree or ancestry, or on someone's acceptance or approval, or even upon a husband's will; it required only that we believe and receive. Anyone who does that, John says, has "the right to become children of God". It's ironic that the baby whose own family was plagued by questions of legitimacy, whose mother was pregnant out of wedlock under questionable circumstances, has the power to adopt us into God's family.

The Word, who humbled himself and gave up his own rights, lifted us up and gave us ours. He opened the doors to the palace and invited us in. As a result, we can be God's children, fully vested in His family, and joint heirs to everything in His kingdom. We will celebrate this and every Christmas with the King! The Word made us part of God's family, with all the attendant rights and privileges. In him, we stand to inherit everything that is rightfully his. Funny—in a way, since he was born so far away from and separated from his Father, Jesus himself was a bit of an orphan, raised in a loving foster home. He knew what it was like to be near and yet far away, to be surrounded by family but still somewhat alone...yet the only begotten Son of God still made a way for every one of us to join him as one of God's children. I'm sure if you ever feel a bit lonely or disconnected this holiday season, he knows just how you feel. He's invited you into the palace, not as a servant but an equal. If you'd like to sit at the family table, he's saved a place for you. Believe. Receive.

Adopted into the Royal Family

He never had a scepter, or wore a royal crown;
He never slept on silken sheets, with servants all around.
Jesus never held a court, or walked the halls of state;
He didn't do the things that politicians think are great.
He never had a palace or the rich material things,
Although he was the Prince of Peace, the very King of kings...
His Kingdom wasn't of this world, and built on war and greed,
But built upon his Father's love, where he is Lord indeed.
And where the earthly system has degraded us and stopped us,
This king used his authority to love us and adopt us!
There's just one catch: to be adopted, you must first believe Him,
And you'll be in His family as soon as you receive Him!

17 Glorious Christmas!

December 17   The Glorious Word, Made in the Likeness of Men

"The Word was made flesh, and dwelt among us, (and we beheld his glory, the glory as of the only begotten of the Father,) full of grace and truth." (John 1:14, KJV) The Word, preexistent from the beginning, the creative force behind the universe, was made flesh. As Paul put it, Jesus "made himself of no reputation, took upon himself the form of a servant, and was made in the likeness of men..." (Philippians 2:7). And oh yeah, he was born like all men, tiny and fragile and vulnerable. He was helpless and hungry and had to be protected like any other baby. He cried, snuggled and nursed. He grew in wisdom and stature over time, in the manner of men, and is the only man to truly understand the phrase "Heaven on Earth".

Jesus created a new and unthinkable paradigm for the Creator: He became part of his own creation. You might expect God to be cosmic and majestic and distant, but instead he used his humanity as a vessel to dwell among us, to share our sorrows, our hopes, our emotions, our experience. Jesus had a personality. He hung out with friends. He went to parties and out to dinner! He smiled, laughed and told stories around the campfire out by the lake. He wept. He taught and healed among us, and rebuked those who made a mockery of his Father's intentions.

In the midst of carnal, selfish men, he offered something we rarely see: the glory of God. He reflected wisdom and grace, and confounded people who expected him to be normal. It was not majestic physical glory, or awesome splendor, it was God's amazing glory transmitted in a smile or a Word. Have you had any glimpses of God's glory lately? We probably have some preconceived notions about glory that keep us from noticing it sometimes, or that cause us to miss it altogether.

In Luke 2:9 the shepherds responded to heavenly glory much as any of us would: "An angel of the Lord appeared to them, and the glory of the Lord shone around them, and they were terrified." Glory can be pretty overwhelming, and we probably most often think of it on a cosmic scale. I know we see it in sunsets and mountaintop vistas, and when we gaze into the night skies, but it's not often we see it literally in someone else. Take a minute to stop thinking of it in grandiose, majestic terms, and think of seeing it reflected in a person.

When you think of beholding God's glory, who do you think of? I know I think of my wife, Nancy, and the love and grace she has extended to me over the years; I see it in my children and grandchildren, who are to me living expressions of God's love and hope for the future...I have seen it at church, moving chairs or rocking a baby in the nursery. I have seen it at Young Life camps, touching lives and offering glimpses of what's to come. And I still see it in the Word of God, preserved for me in John's marvelous narrative, reflected in Moses' law, expounded upon in Paul's amazing letters, and passionately expressed in David's Psalms. Have you looked into the Word of God lately; have you beheld his glory? Have you seen God's glory reflected in a friend or family member? And by the way, did you notice it this Christmas season among the Santas and the snowmen and all of the Christmas displays? You may have walked or driven right by it today! (HINT: it was tiny, and it was probably lying in a manger somewhere as Mary and Joseph hovered over it protectively...)

Glory in a Manger

It's more than what you've read, or heard.
Encounter this: the glorious Word,
The Bible, just not in a book,
But in a PERSON! Take a look
At all it says and you will see
Not Words, but personality.
It's how he smiled, and where he walked,
What Jesus did, and how he talked;
It's healing hands and promises kept,
It's how he prayed, and when he wept...
The Word saw Adam's fatal flaw,
The Word was Moses and the Law.
David praised the Word with song!
Paul presents Him, clear and strong,
The glorious word who came to earth
Disguised in a humble baby's birth...
So, pay attention to this rhyme,
And look for Him this Christmastime.

18 Full Of Gace and Truth
December 18   Look at Truth and Find Grace

John says that we beheld the glory of that baby born in Bethlehem, and that he was "full of grace and truth." I am willing to compliment a friend, and it's good to say something nice about someone, but I can't really recall ever saying, "Old Charlie is a good guy. He's full of grace and truth!" I've known people who were graceful, and I've known folks who were honest, but I've never described someone I knew really well as the absolute repository of veracity. Usually when we say, "He's full of it", we are NOT talking about grace and truth...

Is it possible to say anything more descriptive and astounding about someone? John had observed Jesus at close range for at least 3 years, and certainly knew him well enough to be aware of any flaws he had to contradict this statement. Perhaps John is here echoing the claim Jesus made which was recorded in chapter 14: "I am the way, the truth, and the life. No man comes to the Father, but by me." Jesus said, "I am the truth", and John BELIEVED him.

In an era when journalists (who were once bastions of truth and objectivity) publish sensational stories and suppositions without checking facts, or present part of a story as all of the story, someone who personifies the Truth is rare indeed. In our culture, spin is more common than fact. Advertising agencies present stories and scenarios that will subtly convince you to believe whatever they claim about their products (even if those claims have no basis in reality). In an era where truth is watered down, twisted, and manipulated, truth is an endangered species. Think about this: almost every commercial message you hear or see here at Christmas-time either makes claims that are not true, or creates a virtual myth-like environment in an attempt to alter what you think about reality. Christmas shoppers can avoid black Friday crowds and "save thousands" by buying a car. Shaving commercials show guys lathered up like Santa with a shaving cream beard, when only about 1/3 of that amount of shaving cream is needed to actually shave. In the commercial, if a guy uses a certain cologne, women go nuts over him. In reality a good smelling nerd is still a nerd. In the ads, beer drinkers are all hot, slim young people for whom life is a party (and Alpine climbers live in the cooler to bring up some cold ones from the pristine mountain waters.) I know a few beer drinkers whose actual profile is somewhat different, and up in the mountains you can't even drink the stream water because you might get infected with Giardia, a particularly stubborn and nasty little parasite...

Messages on social media are full of outright balderdash presented as fact, or partial and biased stories that pretend to be the whole truth. Based on the amount of exposure we have to advertising, you hear WAY more lies every day than you hear truth. Even if you don't believe the myths they are throwing at you 100%, the ads are designed to move your needle just a little bit over towards their version of reality. Joseph Goebbels, Hitler's Minister of Propaganda, said "If you repeat a lie often enough, it becomes the truth." Ironically, that's still true. In a world filled with subtlety and spin, be careful that your needle isn't moved too far by falsehood. I'd say this: find truth in your world; read it, listen to it, cultivate it, and rejoice in it. If Jesus was the truth, as he claimed to be, he is worth far more of your time than all of the newscasts, FB posts and commercial messages you will ever hear. And I'm willing to bet that if you listen to truth, you will also find grace.

The Truth About Grace

The truth about lies is they're hard to see,
Bombarding us from everywhere,
Reshaping our reality
with subtle falsehoods that we share...
Lies come at us from every place—
From ads that do more than they seem—
Convincing us to load our face
with three shaves worth of shaving cream!
We're surrounded by these lies
from cradle through impetuous youth
While subtle Falsehood in disguise
disparages important Truth.
Grab hold of Truth! Don't let it go,
And don't let Falsehood take its place;
Beauty may be Truth, but know
That more importantly, Truth is Grace.
Stay away from falsehood and its danger
As you enjoy the greetings of the season;
For truth and grace are lying in a manger:
It's Christmas time, and Jesus is the reason.

19 Christmas Coincidences
December 19   Wow, what Are the Odds?

"In those days Caesar Augustus issued a decree that a census should be taken of the entire Roman world. (This was the first census that took place while Quirinius was governor of Syria.) And everyone went to their own town to register. So Joseph also went up from the town of Nazareth in Galilee to Judea, to Bethlehem the town of David, because he belonged to the house and line of David." (Luke 2:1-4 NIV)

Joseph was from Nazareth, not Bethlehem. Under normal circumstances, Jesus should have been born there at home in Nazareth, a relatively sleepy little village in Galilee. But a taxation decree from Caesar Augustus forced Joseph to take Mary from Galilee to Bethlehem, and it was there Jesus was born. This fulfilled a prediction written over 700 years before by the prophet Micah: "But you, Bethlehem Ephrata, though you are small among the clans of Judah, out of you will come for me one who will be ruler over Israel, whose origins are from of old, from ancient times." (Micah 5:2 NIV).

Look at a couple of things about these verses: First, the birth of Jesus was a REAL event that took place in a REAL location in the midst of REAL historical events. There was a census (you can look it up), and Quirinius was actually a mid-level governor in Judea. (Scholars place his time of service and the Roman census both at somewhere around 6 AD, which helps to date the birth of Christ relative to events from that time.)

Second, because Joseph went from Nazareth to Bethlehem to be registered, Jesus was born away from his childhood home. Since Jesus grew up in Nazareth, the Pharisees did not associate him later on with Bethlehem, and it was one of the things that bothered them about Jesus and kept them from seeing him as the Messiah. He wasn't from the religious and cultural center of Jerusalem, and it diminished his importance in their eyes. In John 7:41-42 they argued about it: "But some said, "Will the Christ come out of Galilee? Has not the Scripture said that the Christ comes from the seed of David and from the town of Bethlehem, where David was?"

The Pharisees (like Herod's elders who consulted the Magi in Matthew 2) knew that the Messiah would come from the city of David, and their tribal knowledge presumed that Jesus grew up in Nazareth. What they didn't realize was that out of all the places in all of Judea, Joseph had to leave Galilee and travel with his pregnant wife to Bethlehem, and the timing had to be such that she delivered not at home in Nazareth but while staying briefly in the city of David. Pretty remarkable that a Roman decree moved Hebrew people around so that Joseph and Mary ended up in Bethlehem, the exact birthplace of the Messiah, which fulfilled Micah's prediction from over 700 years before... Remarkable? Yes. Coincidence? **No**

The Actual Story of Christmas Began Much Earlier

You don't think He created earth; you can't believe the Virgin birth.

His parables and works were fine, but you don't see him as divine.

Perhaps if you could look and see the Hebrew Scriptures' prophecy,

You'd come to find it all makes sense: if there was one coincidence,

Then you could push him out of mind, or call me intellectually blind;

But search the Scriptures, and you'll find

A dozen prophecies aligned with things that Christ would do.

So was he God? Or was it just a coincidence or two?

A dozen? No, I think I undershot,

since actually there really are a LOT—

Just take that Bible down from off the shelf,

And do some research. Look it up yourself!

Those prophecies from hundreds of years before;

I've quoted a few, but there are many more.

The are some folks who say it can't make sense;

But I don't think it was coincidence!

20 From the Hillsides into Heaven
December 20   A Humble Start to an Amazing Story

"And there were shepherds living out in the fields nearby, keeping watch over their flocks at night. An angel of the Lord appeared to them, and the glory of the Lord shone around them, and they were terrified. But the angel said to them, "Do not be afraid. I bring you good news that will cause great joy for all the people." (Luke 2:8-10 NIV)

Normally if a King was coming into the world, it would have been in a palace, and there would have been great fanfare over the birth of an heir to the throne. News would have been sent out from the palace with trumpets and proclamations so that everyone could hear the big news! Royal family members and political insiders would have been the first to hear the news, and it would have spread from there.

In Luke's account about the new-born king, however, the news did not come from the palace but from the pasture, sent to a group that was more often than not marginalized by religious society. Even in God's economy, this did not seem like a logical choice. Shepherds were not the first group almost anybody would have picked to receive the good news of Jesus' birth. (Why not priests or soldiers, or somebody from the palace?) Any Messiah maker with good sense would have proclaimed the news of the Savior's arrival to the High Priest, or a governor, or someone with influence and a platform; maybe somebody who could get the news on TV.

Why was Jesus born then and there, before God could take advantage of all of our modern conveyances? Looking back, doesn't it seem like God used really poor judgment in His timing for the Advent? As it was written in "Jesus Christ, Superstar": "You'd have managed better if you had it planned; why'd you choose such a backward time and such a strange land? If you'd have come today you would have reached a whole nation; Israel in 4 BC had no mass communication."

Why was Jesus born in such a primitive time? Why did God choose to send angels out into the countryside to announce the news to mere shepherds? Some say they were loners, always out by themselves following sheep around. It was a humble job away from the limelight. Some also say shepherds were not the most social of guys, maybe not too high on the Bethlehem social ladder, and not the first guys you'd invite home to dinner...

On the other hand, David was a shepherd, and he developed pretty fair fighting skills, wrote songs and Psalms, and ended up having a pretty notable career. I think the angel appeared to shepherds as a subtle nod to Jesus' ancestry, and as a reminder that great things can have humble beginnings. They carried the "good news that will cause great joy" into town and out to the surrounding areas; out of the hillsides and into history. And you know what? They may not have had TV or the internet, but amazingly enough the shepherds' story is still being told, and is well known in today's modern media age... Perhaps God knew what He was doing after all by announcing the good news when and where He did!

Two things: does this good news bring you great joy? (I hope so!) *And who are you telling about it?* Perhaps someone you know is waiting to be carried from the hillsides into history. And into heaven as well.

Certain Poor Shepherds

There, on the hills near Bethlehem, the plaintive, restless flock
Was destined for Jerusalem as sacrificial stock.
Trying to sleep on a fitful night, We heard a sound--almost took flight—
Awakened by a glorious light, astounded by the startling sight
Of a messenger whose voice instills
Great fear, and brought us shepherds chills
Out there, alone up in the hills...
He gave us tidings of great joy!
"There is a King! A newborn boy!
They'll call his name Immanuel!"
With that, a choir began to swell
And sing of glory, peace as well,
As we were captive to its spell:
He told us, then, to go and tell...

Well after that, what could we do?
We went! We found the babe! It's true!
Of all the things I've done, and not done yet,
That is the thing I can't --I won't-- forget.
Whatever I may do, or men may say,
Say this: I was in Bethlehem that day,
And saw the child, and the manger where he lay.

21 The Nativity That Never Was
December 21   Sorry, but Most Nativity Scenes are WRONG

"Now there were in the same country shepherds living out in the fields, keeping watch over their flock by night." (Luke 2:8, NIV) "And when they [the wise men] had come into the house, they saw the young Child with Mary His mother, and fell down and worshiped Him." (Matthew 2:11, NIV) I've always loved the nativity scenes, with the animals, shepherds and wise men gathered around the manger honoring the baby Jesus, while an angel hovers over the stable as Joseph and Mary look on...

The problem is, that scene never happened. The traditional nativity scenes are based on a couple of different events that took place at least several months but up to two years apart, each with a different location and set of players. I guess you could say that Nativity scenes are Cliff Notes' representations that portray both events together...

The only group who made it to the manger area out behind the inn when Jesus was born were the shepherds. Once they got over their fright somewhere out in the Judean countryside, the shepherds did indeed stop by the manger in Bethlehem; but it was shortly AFTER being visited by an angel. (That angel, by the way, was joined by a host of other Angels who sang in celebration.) So, contrary to most Nativity scenes, it wasn't a single angel, it was many; and the angel didn't go into town with the Shepherds to the manger. It says in Luke 2:15 that the angels "went back into heaven." The shepherds went into town on their own, where they found "Mary and Joseph, and the baby lying in a manger." They were pretty fired up when they realized that something pretty big was going on, and that they were part of it! Luke 2:20 says they "returned, glorifying and praising God for all the things they had heard and seen, which were just as they had been told."

The shepherds, it seems, have a lot in common with us. They are ordinary folks. They heard some really good news. They had a choice: ignore the news, stay out in the fields, and just go on with their lives as if nothing had happened; or they could believe the message, go and find out more about this baby, and meet him face to face. You have the same information the shepherds did, and the exact same choice. Something pretty big is going on. Be part of it.

The REAL Nativity Scene

Nativity scenes are quite profound,
With shepherds and Magi gathered 'round,
Adoring Jesus, meek and mild...
The angel greets this new-born child
With Mary and Joseph and all the rest.
But it doesn't pass the Bible test!
Just look at the Nativity: It isn't accurate history,
And if you give it scrutiny, you'll find it's more of a summary.
And that's ok, just get it right: Some history was made that night
Since all of those events occurred,
Just not the way you've always heard.
The shepherds on the hillside heard
The Angel speak his glorious word,
Then ran to town without delay
To where the baby Jesus lay.
That's when the angels came to sing
Of Glory to the Newborn King!
The Magi visited later on,
When everybody else was gone.
They didn't hear the Angels' song,
So most Nativity scenes are wrong...
Before your nose gets out of joint,
I'm not being critical; here's my point:
I'm not saying it's kinda lame
The Nativity scene is not the same;
The important thing is, Jesus came!
Although it may lack accuracy,
The scene at the Nativity has elements of history
Presented as a summary for which there is no mystery.
Nativity scenes may not be totally factual,
But Jesus came. That truth is totally actual.

22 Herod's Legacy

December 22   Real People. Real Christmas. Real Danger.

"After Jesus was born in Bethlehem in Judea, during the time of King Herod, Magi from the east came to Jerusalem and asked, "Where is the one who has been born king of the Jews? We saw his star when it rose and have come to worship him." When King Herod heard this he was disturbed, and all Jerusalem with him..." (Matthew 2:1-3, NIV)

The Magi, who studied the heavens and knew something about the arrival of a new king of the Jews, came "from the east" to find out about this newly born king... Naturally they went first to the current king in Jerusalem, Herod the Great—a cruel man who was known for high taxes and building the glorious temple. His accomplishments as King were impressive, and he was the most prolific builder in all of Israel's history. He was in perhaps the last year of his reign, dying from gonorrhea and possibly cancer. He had a long, tumultuous reign filled with treachery and murder. He not only executed his wife, Miriamne, but her mother Alexandra as well. He had two of his brothers-in-law killed, and also executed his own sons Alexander, Aristobulus, and Antipater. He was so jealous of his throne that at one point it prompted Augustus to say, "It is better to be Herod's pig than Herod's son" (a reference to the fact that the pig had a better chance for survival than a son, since Herod's household didn't eat pork).

Matthew's description of Herod's reaction to the Magi is intriguing. While there is much to explore about the Magi, it is also interesting to take a closer look at Herod's role in the nativity. After all, he was at least partly responsible for sending them to Jesus. His scheme did not work out the way he intended. "Then Herod called the Magi secretly and found out from them the exact time the star had appeared. He sent them to Bethlehem and said, "Go and search carefully for the child. As soon as you find him, report to me, so that I too may go and worship him." (Matthew 2:7-8)

Herod is a somewhat forgotten part of this nativity, and he certainly played a significant role in the birth and early life of Jesus. Matthew says in verse 3 that when the Magi arrived in Jerusalem, "Herod was troubled, and all Jerusalem with him." It might make sense that Herod was troubled—he guarded his throne zealously, and certainly did not enjoy having other aspiring kings around. But why was all Jerusalem troubled with him? Dr. Duane Edward Spencer taught that since Herod was a cruel ruler who was not exactly beloved in Jerusalem, the fact that the city was disturbed along with him at the approach of these men suggested a somewhat larger and more capable party than three men on camels—perhaps a troop of famed Persian cavalry. It makes sense, since a few men carrying valuable gifts would have been easy prey for robbers, and three guys on camels probably wouldn't make a city tremble. This is a real story about real people, and it makes sense that men of this stature would not travel without protection, and that Herod and people in Jerusalem would all have their own interpretation of events.

Herod tried to twist the Magi to his own ends, asking them to go find this newborn king so he could "worship him". Like many politicians before and since, Herod was lying about his true intent. He was a paranoid ruler who was constantly involved in intrigue and questionable choices. (A Herod played a role in Jesus' birth and in his death. His son, Herod Antipas, carried on the family tradition of making poor choices by marrying his half-brother's wife, Herodias. She was the one whose daughter danced provocatively for him and then demanded the head of John the Baptist. Definitely soap opera material... Herod Antipas is the same guy who wanted Jesus to perform for him, and who sent him back to Pilate after a very cursory "trial").

But at about the time of Jesus' birth, Herod the Great sent the Magi to Bethlehem to find Jesus and report back to him. When they didn't bring him a report, he reacted by doing something that followed his reputation down the corridors of time. He killed all the male children in Bethlehem two years of age and under. While he missed Jesus, his cruelty touched many other lives, and has always been known as the "Slaughter of the Innocents." Real people. Real events. Know your history: Jesus was really actually part of it.

The Rest of the Christmas Story

The Holidays are twinkling lights
And carolers on snowy nights,
Our Christmas movies on TV and presents underneath the tree.
We think of things we love so much—
The Christmas tree, the gifts and such,
And little children's shining eyes with every Santa Claus surprise!
But don't forget at Christmas, when your stockings and hearts are filled,
The boys in Bethlehem, and the evil king who had them killed.
Traditions and gifts are nice, and so are all the things we feel—
But don't forget the little boys. Yeah, Christmas just got real.

23 Herod the Not So Great
December 23   **H**e's **E**vidently **R**eally **O**bviously **D**epraved

"When [Herod] had called together all the people's chief priests and teachers of the law, he asked them where the Messiah was to be born. "In Bethlehem in Judea," they replied, "for this is what the prophet has written: "'But you, Bethlehem, in the land of Judah, are by no means least among the rulers of Judah; for out of you will come a ruler who will shepherd my people Israel.' (Matthew 2:4-6, NIV). Herod acted like he was helping these wise men from the East, but he was actually trying to use them for his own ends. Probably because of his declining health, Herod stayed and sent them to find out where the Christ was located so that he could then eliminate this new threat to his throne. We'll look at the Wise Men a little closer tomorrow. But, "When Herod realized that he had been outwitted by the Magi, he was furious, and he gave orders to kill all the boys in Bethlehem and its vicinity who were two years old and under, in accordance with the time he had learned from the Magi. Then what was said through the prophet Jeremiah was fulfilled: "A voice is heard in Ramah, weeping and great mourning, Rachel weeping for her children and refusing to be comforted, because they are no more." (Matthew 2:16-18, NIV).

This is when the birth of Jesus started getting REAL, ya'll. Herod murdered a bunch of young boys in Bethlehem, just playing the odds and assuming that he would catch this newborn king among them. He chose two years and under because some time had passed since he sent the Magi to Bethlehem and then waited for their return, so a number of babies were killed in his attempt to eliminate the threat to his power. Reliable estimates suggest anywhere from six to twenty children would have been murdered by Herod's men. (Hmm, I wonder if these men covered their identities and wielded swords.) This despicable act—not so different than some of the things we read about in the paper today—became known as "the slaughter of the innocents", and has been questioned by historians because it was not widely mentioned in extra-Biblical sources. However, historian R. T. France, addressing the story's absence in "Antiquities of the Jews", argues that "the murder of a few infants in a small village [is] not on a scale to match the more spectacular assassinations recorded by Josephus". After all, Herod killed people who were well known in Jerusalem—including his wife, mother-in-law, brother-in-law, and three of his own sons—so the act of killing a few unknown infants out in a small village may not have been front page news at the time...

This event is still today one of the main things we remember about Herod the Great—and one of the great tragedies connected with the birth of Jesus. Yes, his birth is good news, tidings of great joy. But amazingly enough, a baby who could save the world and who would teach nothing but love had evil and implacable foes, men who would kill rather than acknowledge him. I've always felt like the persistent hatred and vitriol about Christ (don't people use his name to swear?) actually validates his identity. If he was just a passing nobody, he would have been forgotten long ago, as forgotten as the Scribes and Pharisees who argued with him in the temple. The fact that so many folks from both now and then resist him so vehemently makes me think that there are larger spiritual stakes involved, and that he must have been something more than a pretty good rabbi. There was passionate resistance against Jesus, enemies who would twist words and commit murder to keep him from fulfilling his mission. There were men who bristled at the very name of Jesus, who didn't want it mentioned or valued. This Christmas season, people here in America are demanding that manger scenes be removed, and that Christ be taken out of Christmas. After all these years, men are still trying to eliminate the baby Jesus. Some things, it seems, never change...

What's a King to DO?

The winter had been hard; so, when they showed up at the gate,
Armed to the teeth and sitting horse, of course I made them wait.
Their coming caught us all off guard. And yet they brought that news,
Something about a star they'd seen, and a new king of the Jews...
My counselors confirmed the Scriptures also contained some clues:
The rumor was, a king would rise somewhere in Bethlehem;
I must admit my humor was not the best it's ever been,
Confronted with these Magi and their horses, and their men...
But I kept my composure, sent them out, told them to bring
Me any information they could find about this king--
This tiny new usurper who would dare to steal my throne!
My family learned when they could not leave well enough alone,
That Herod is not pleased with other applicants to his court:
I'll see to it this infant's reign--just like his life--is short.
This little king, his family and all the world will learn
How Herod treats his rivals, when the Wise Men all return...

24 The Magi
December 24   Probably Why they call them Wise Men

"After they had heard the king, they went on their way, and the star they had seen when it rose went ahead of them until it stopped over the place where the child was. When they saw the star, they were overjoyed. On coming to the house, they saw the child with his mother Mary, and they bowed down and worshiped him. Then they opened their treasures and presented him with gifts of gold, frankincense and myrrh. And having been warned in a dream not to go back to Herod, they returned to their country by another route. (Matthew 2:9-12, NIV)

Most Nativity scenes show 3 wise men at the manger, and Christmas lore is rich with images of and legends about them. The Magi are a fascinating part of the Christmas story, with their camels and trappings and gifts, and they deserve some study because of their place in the series of events spoken of in Matthew. They are mysterious figures, thought by some to be kings of Persia, or possibly Zoroastrian priests who studied the stars as part of their religion.

It has also been suggested that perhaps they descended from Jews who had been exiled to Persia but rose to positions of prominence, (think: Daniel, or perhaps Esther and Mordecai) which might explain their familiarity with OT prophecy about the Messiah. We sometimes forget that the ancients had clearer views of the night skies than we do (no city lights to cloud their view), and plenty of time on their hands (no sitcoms or prime time TV to distract them). The average shepherd probably knew as much about the position and movement of the heavens as some current astronomers do, and the Magi grew up studying the stars religiously.

Trivia facts about them: 1. Nowhere does the Bible mention only 3 wise men; there are 3 gifts, brought by Magi. 2. It is highly unlikely that there were 3 guys traveling on camels. With gifts of such value, there had to be a group large enough to protect itself, and they probably had some soldiers or cavalry with them... 3. They didn't make it to the manger. At the time of Christ's birth, they were probably approaching Jerusalem to talk to Herod. They could have also gone to Caesarea by the Sea, where one of Herod's palaces was located. 4. Lots of folks have tried to associate the star with a known astronomical event, and there may have been one initially; but at the end, since the star rose and led them to the child, it is likely that it was a unique manifestation, such as God's radiance in the Shekinah, that provided guidance for the last leg of their journey. 5. They saw not a baby, but a young child (clear difference in the original Greek), and came to a house, not a stable. Jesus was weeks if not months old when they presented their gifts... 6. The tradition of our Christmas gift giving comes at least partially from the gifts of the Magi. Like them, we should bring what we have and lay it at the feet of Jesus! 7. Joseph isn't mentioned here, which doesn't mean he wasn't around, just that he wasn't mentioned. (He is around later when Jesus is 12 and they find him teaching in the temple).

Finally, after seeing the young boy and worshipping him, they returned home by another route. My BSU Director Glen Norris used to teach the version that said, "*They went home another way*." He always maintained that anyone who really meets Jesus, and truly worships him, will be fundamentally changed by that experience, and *go home another way*, changed from how they were before. So the wise men not only took another route, they became different types of men, fulfilled by faith and encouraged by events. As result, they went home with new perspective, new motivation, and new direction. My Christmas prayer is that our world could open the true gift of Christmas and do the same thing. As you reflect on the origins of Christmas, may you, too, be wise.

(Even though I know there weren't three Wise Men on camels at the manger, I wrote this following poem anyway, a different perspective on the birth of Christ, its very unique set of circumstances and the players presented in the traditional Nativities...)

The Camel

Slow he rises! Hideous, hairy: hollowly he plods his course:
His hump-backed and misshapen body carries its express remorse.
Glaring eyes with bushy eyebrows-- stinking, spitting, ugly beast!
Of all mankind's domestic creatures, he must be the very least.
Men for centuries have mocked him: used, abused him without care-
Silently he bears their scorn, ungainly walks the earth aware
Of comfort in his secret: "Fools! These men will never know
That once, I heard the baby's cry, saw where the star did go,
And brought my magi bearing gifts, and watched them bowing low."

25 Christmas Gifts

December 25   Christmas Comes Just Once a Year... Doesn't It?

Christmas is all about giving and opening gifts! It is a tradition that goes back to the gifts of the Magi, which were presented to Jesus as a young child sometime after he was born. Some folks relate it to Saturnalia, a pagan Roman festival which pre-dated the birth of Christ, and which was supplanted by the Christian celebration of Jesus' birth. Since people gave each other small gifts during that winter festival, the custom was appropriated by early Church Fathers. Which gift will be your favorite this year?

We commemorate the actions of the Magi in Matthew 2:11: "And when they had come into the house, they saw the young Child with Mary His mother, and fell down and worshiped Him. And when they had opened their treasures, they presented gifts to Him: gold, frankincense, and myrrh."

Gifts are a wonderful part of our Christmas celebration. But as you open your presents today, remember that there are gifts, and then there are GIFTS:

There is the gift of life.

There is the gift of love.

And then there's this: "For the wages of sin is death; but the GIFT of God is eternal life through Jesus Christ our Lord." (Romans 6:23, KJV).

"For by grace you have been saved through faith, and that not of yourselves. It is the GIFT of God, not of works, lest any man should boast." (Ephesians 2:8-9, KJV).

"But the free GIFT is not like the offense. For if by the one man's offense many died, much more the grace of God and the GIFT by the grace of the one Man, Jesus Christ, abounded unto many." (Romans 5:15, NIV)

"For God so loved the world that he GAVE his only begotten son, that whosoever believes in him should not perish, but have everlasting life." (John 3:16, KJV)

No matter where you are and no matter what your circumstances today, never forget that Christmas is not about toys or things. It's about new life. And it's about a new KIND of life. To me, eternal life is an attitude that not only transcends time and space but it begins here and now! I like to think it is what Gus McCrae meant in "Lonesome Dove": "It ain't dying I'm talking about, it's **living**. I doubt it matters where you die, but it matters where you LIVE."

Gus had a point, and I'm pretty sure he intended to enjoy life every day. So should we.

This year, don't limit Christmas gifts to a single day. Celebrate it all year long! Embrace life wherever you are. Live with an awareness of the gifts that matter. Don't get so caught up in your new iPhone that you miss the greatest gift of all! Merry Christmas!

A Christmas Rhyme for Christmas Time

Sing Hosanna, peace on earth! Celebrate the Savior's birth!
As Angels sing, Rejoice with them! This baby, born in Bethlehem,
Made every earthly power shift, and offered us His matchless gift.
Give "Peace on earth" and spread "Good Cheer"!
But tell me, if this isn't clear:
Since Jesus showed that "God came near",
why celebrate just once a year?
In winter, summer, spring, and fall, open the greatest gift of all—
At home, abroad, at work or play—Celebrate Christmas every day!
Whenever you recall this rhyme: it's Him, it's you, it's Christmas time!

26 Real Christmas. Real Danger

December 26   The Creepiest Christmas Ever

"When they had gone, an angel of the Lord appeared to Joseph in a dream. "Get up," he said, "take the child and his mother and escape to Egypt. Stay there until I tell you, for Herod is going to search for the child to kill him." So he got up, took the child and his mother during the night and left for Egypt, where he stayed until the death of Herod. And so was fulfilled what the Lord had said through the prophet: "Out of Egypt I called my son." (Matthew 2:12-15, NIV).

The Christmas story doesn't end with the Nativity. It begins there. For Joseph and Mary, it meant a hasty departure under cover of darkness to a strange land. It meant hard travel in open country with a young mother and a toddler, whom Herod was seeking to kill... Come to think of it, it had to be a scary trip, maybe the scariest road trip experience of all time. Yes, there was an aging and jealous king trying to eliminate a potential threat to his throne, but it wasn't just *Herod* who wanted the baby dead.

Paul reminded us in Ephesians 6:12 "For we do not wrestle against flesh and blood, but against principalities, against powers, against the rulers of the darkness of this age, against spiritual hosts of wickedness in the heavenly places..." Not only Herod, but *every dark power in this world* had to be uneasy, sensing this sudden goodness which was now present on planet earth. Surely every evil force could feel a shudder of its own death knell, and stirred blindly and restlessly, reacting with vague disquiet against God's work in the world.

Against a creepier background than any horror film could conjure up, Joseph took his little family and set out for Egypt. Satan has never been omniscient, or he surely would have known who this baby was in advance, and ended it all at the manger... But the foolishness of God is wiser than the wisdom of evil. Undoubtedly, through the millennia, Satan was anticipating the arrival of a coming king, and was ready to do battle with God's royal emissary and savior. Perhaps, like the Pharisees, he was looking for a majestic, powerful king who would come heralded in glory, ready to fight the Romans. He certainly worked hard in the courts of both Judean kings and Roman emperors (and most royal houses throughout history), using ego and treachery to corrupt and contaminate almost everyone who attained a position of strength. Winston Churchill, who was a pretty astute chronicler of history, said "Power corrupts; absolute power corrupts absolutely."

The devil has been pretty effective at corrupting leaders (he's still doing it today), but Satan did not foresee God's unusual plan. God chose weakness to confound strength. He heralded not a military kingdom but a spiritual one. Against all power-hungry logic, He sent humility to oppose power. God chose a frail baby to end an evil empire based on selfishness and pride; and He sent Jesus to begin a **new** one based on peace and love. Guess where it starts, the day after Christmas? Look no further than your own heart...

Fitful Dreams

Forced to flee in the dead of night,
Joseph had disturbing dreams
Which warned him that they must take flight
From Herod's mad and murderous schemes.

Commanded by his jealous word,
Assassins through their village crept,
And performed their duties undeterred
As mothers wailed and fathers wept.

But Herod's minions missed the mark,
As Joseph took his wife and infant son
Traveling hard to safety in the dark:
Their long and dangerous journey had begun.

And every evil power on this earth
Was restless as it sensed this new-born king,
Uneasy since the announcement and the birth,
Uncertain of the changes it would bring.

The powers of darkness felt the child's great good,
Felt the Spirit around him as it flowed,
And stirred to end this danger, if they could,
These pilgrims alone, out on the open road...

27 Walking By Faith Is No Picnic
December 27   This Christmas Business is Tougher than you Think

After Herod died, an angel of the Lord appeared in a dream to Joseph in Egypt and said, "Get up, take the child and his mother and go to the land of Israel, for those who were trying to take the child's life are dead." So he got up, took the child and his mother and went to the land of Israel. But when he heard that Archelaus was reigning in Judea in place of his father Herod, he was afraid to go there. Having been warned in a dream, he withdrew to the district of Galilee, and he went and lived in a town called Nazareth. So was fulfilled what was said through the prophets, that he would be called a Nazarene. (Matthew 2:19-23 NIV)

Joseph's relationship with God was not limited to the pre-Advent announcement about his first son. Obviously, he had to deal with issues that were far beyond the scope of most typical first-century Jewish husbands and fathers. He had to deal with a bride who was pregnant before the wedding; the messengers of God coming to him with directions; a pretty dicey political situation, what with the local king trying to kill his son and all; and yeah, he had to make some pretty difficult travel arrangements under adverse circumstances. Then he and Mary also had to decide where to live, and how to raise the Son of God who had been placed under their care. They still had to evaluate neighborhoods and make assessments about what was happening and where to live.

I think it's interesting that, even under the protection of the Most-High God, Joseph and Mary still had to make decisions about where to go; they still had to take action to be obedient. They weren't beamed magically to Egypt, but had to take flight in the dead of night. Yes, they had been warned of Herod's treachery, but they still had to get up and escape to Egypt, to live among strangers in a strange land. Traveling that far in those days was no easy task, particularly with an infant on the trip. They were certainly vulnerable and in danger, but they trusted God and responded to His word.

I'm sure that those weeks were lonely and fearful, and that there were moments of doubt and uncertainty for the young couple as they began their life together. Perhaps there is something in their story for us. A walk with God is not a magical Union that takes place in spiritual realms; it is a journey through hard times in an uncertain world where bad things can happen. It is not sitting on a cloud and enjoying a life of ease, but it involves acting in faith while being obedient to God's word.

I think it's instructive that Mary and Joseph:
1) listened to God's word to them;
2) made decisions based on what He said; and
3) demonstrated obedience to God by acting upon his instruction. Their obedience involved leaving home, planning a last-minute trip, and taking steps into uncertainty. (Without a car-seat, a Pack-N-Play, or even an aisle seat in economy class.) They listened to what God said and they DID it. You think maybe we could learn from that?

A Journey of Faith

I hope these dreams are who they say they are;
  We've left our family, and we've traveled far
    To live down here in Egypt. It's been rough,
      (As if this birth had not been hard enough!)
        So now we have to take a different tack;
          The angel says that we should travel back!
          Judea isn't safe; so, where to go?
            I guess when we get closer, we will know...
          But Mary is amazing. We will make it,
        And if God has some more advice, we'll take it.
      We're only strangers living in this land—
    A circumstance I never would have planned—
  But we have both obeyed the Lord's command:
So in Him we will trust, and take our stand.

28 A Father's Love

The logical Biblical extension of the Nativity would be Christ's boyhood; but Scripture offers us little to explore. There is, however, this nugget:

"Then he went down to Nazareth with them and was obedient to them. But his mother treasured all these things in her heart. And Jesus grew in wisdom and stature, and in favor with God and man." (Luke 2:51-52 NIV)

It's a little intriguing to think about Jesus as a boy, and we can speculate about what he must have been like. Certainly, he was normal and polite, and we do know that by age twelve he exhibited remarkable poise and wisdom... But there are not a whole lot of other details given in the Bible about his childhood. Comedians have always joked that it must have been tough being Jesus' sibling, since you would always hear, "Why can't you be like Jesus? HE behaves!"

In the Apocryphal gospel of Thomas, the boy Jesus is depicted as performing some whimsical miracles, which is probably why that book stayed apocryphal and didn't become part of the Canon. But in point of fact, not much is written about the boy Jesus, except for Luke's anecdote about Jesus staying behind at the temple at age 12 while his parents headed back to Galilee...

Jesus was obviously gifted as a teacher and amazed the scribes and rabbis in the temple; but most of his amazing qualities were kept private, just as Mary "treasured all these things in her heart". If you are a mom or dad, aunt or uncle, or friend of the family, perhaps you have spent time around a toddler or a small child. Think of being amazed at their development. Think of being overwhelmed by little things they do, from imitating you to discovering something with wide-eyed wonder... What things do you observe in little ones and hold secretly as precious memories in your heart? Mary knew those things about Jesus and she treasured them.

As our Heavenly Father, it is entirely possible that God feels the same way about us; He watches our development, he sees us grow from spiritual babes into spiritual toddlers, and he treasures us in his heart. Have you ever equated how your Heavenly Father feels about you with the way you cherish an infant, or laugh at loud at a toddler's antics? I bet He takes the same delight in you, and is just as interested in your growth and development. Your picture is in His wallet; your crude but well-meaning artwork is on His refrigerator. God loves us not just for who we are, but He even knows who we will become as we trust him to help us navigate our path in a complex and fallen world.

Luke says that Jesus grew in four dimensions: mentally, physically, spiritually and socially. Like you, Jesus grew up in the real world. Like you, he was cherished, appreciated, and loved. That's probably a good thing to remember as we head into the New Year. Treasure those things in your heart, and grow.

Treasured

Mary watched as Jesus grew, and marveled at the things he knew;
Beginning with the manger's start, she treasured Jesus in her heart,
Like any mother's heart would do. Did you know someone treasures you?
One who loves to watch you grow, desires to teach you all they know,
One who loves with all His might, and watches you with great delight!
Your Heavenly Father hears your prayers; He listens, and He really cares.
He loves you now, and every minute; His wallet has your picture in it!
He adores your every move, and offers you a Father's love.
By every way it can be measured, understand this:
That You. Are. Treasured.

29 Amazing Then; Amazing Now
December 29   "I Thought he was With YOU!"

"When he was twelve years old, they went up to the festival, according to the custom. After the festival was over, while his parents were returning home, the boy Jesus stayed behind in Jerusalem, but they were unaware of it. Thinking he was in their company, they traveled on for a day. Then they began looking for him among their relatives and friends. When they did not find him, they went back to Jerusalem to look for him. After three days they found him in the temple courts, sitting among the teachers, listening to them and asking them questions. Everyone who heard him was amazed at his understanding and his answers. (Luke 2:42-47 NIV)

This is the only anecdote Luke shared about the boy Jesus, the only real scrap of information we have about his formative years. I have always wondered how he became aware of his supernatural capacity. Did it happen all at once, or bit by bit? Certainly, he was commissioned for public ministry at John's baptism, but we are not really given clarity about exactly when he knew who he was and why he came.

This story offers a couple of clues: first, at age 12 he demonstrated wisdom and comprehension beyond his years, which amazed the teachers at the temple. Men who were able to teach in the temple courts had generally spent a lifetime in the Scriptures and studying at the feet of other rabbis, so the fact that Jesus could astonish such men was no small thing. But interestingly, it says in verse 48 that when his parents saw him, "they were [also] amazed", meaning perhaps they had not really seen such precocity in their son before now...

When Jesus told them he must be about his Father's business, Luke says in verse 50, "they did not understand the statement which He spoke to them." This incident at the temple was new information to Mary and Joseph, and therefore was new behavior on their son's part. I like to think that Jesus enjoyed a fairly normal childhood, playing and learning and growing alongside his brothers and sisters, that his formative years were full of joy and growth and love. (And yes, Jesus had siblings. Mark 3:21 and 31 speak of his mother and brothers seeking him, and in Mark 6:3, the people from the village ask, "Is this not the carpenter, the Son of Mary, and brother of James, Joses, Judas, and Simon? And are not His sisters here with us?") Jesus grew up in fairly large family, playing with his brothers and sisters. Perhaps they played hide and seek in the village, or chunked rocks at a nearby stream.

Somehow, I think that his early years connected him with his creation deepened his compassion for mankind, and contributed to the love and resolve that later carried him through his mission. Russ Massey, a great Bible teacher and my Bible Study Fellowship teaching leader in Conroe, taught logically that if Joseph died fairly soon after this happened, then Jesus would have assumed (as the eldest son) familial responsibilities, helping Mary run the household, and assumed some of the burdens of running a family. It's a fairly logical assumption, one that makes sense.

But I hope that in the years leading up to this he had carefree moments of play and laughter as well, bathed in the love of parents who knew all too well how special he was, waiting and watching to see how the prophecies would come true.

This "I thought he was with you" trip to Jerusalem was probably Mary and Joseph's first big "Aha!" moment that the Time was getting closer at hand, and that Jesus truly was gifted in ways that had been foretold. I wonder if it changed their relationship with him, and what they began to learn about him from that point going forward... When was your first big "Aha!" moment about Jesus? Has it changed your relationship with him, and is there something more you can learn from him going forward? When you see him in a new way, you'll discover (like Joseph and Mary, and the guys at the temple) He is pretty amazing!

The Amazing Twelve-Year-Old

I thought he was with YOU! Or, "Wow, we thought he was with THEM!"
But here they were, a long day's travel from Jerusalem,
And Jesus wasn't there. So, Mary and Joseph turned around
And searched for several days before their precious son was found.
They found him in the temple, calmly sitting there unfazed,
Reasoning with the elders. Everybody was amazed
At all the wisdom he displayed, when all was said and done:
And surely it began to dawn that Jesus was the one.
A page had turned. His parents knew his mission had begun...

30   Don't Miss This Fact About Jesus
December 30   The Obedient God

Hidden away in Luke's comments about Jesus as a boy is a nugget you should not miss: Luke tells the story of the Obedient God. "Why were you searching for me?" he asked. "Didn't you know I had to be in my Father's house?" But they did not understand what he was saying to them. Then he went down to Nazareth with them and was obedient to them..." (Luke 2:49-51 NIV)

Yesterday we talked about this passage from Luke, which tells us pretty much everything we know about the years between Jesus' childhood and manhood. Here are a few final thoughts on Jesus as a boy... There is so little in Scripture to go on about Jesus' boyhood, and it's tempting to try to reconstruct some things, but it is always important to let Scripture be Scripture, and allow the story to speak for itself. Luke 2:52 says that Jesus "grew in wisdom and stature, and in favor with God and men."

He was growing in a balanced way; and the Bible basically says that his development was apparently fairly normal. I love the fact that Luke points out how Jesus grew in four dimensions: mentally, physically, spiritually and socially. He wasn't some spiritual nerd who didn't live in the real world, but there was a balance in his growth that encompassed intelligence, strength, and his relationship with both God and men. That's probably a good template for goal-setting when we start jotting down those New Year's resolutions...

As for this story, the fact that he slipped away and stayed at the temple caught both Mary and Joseph a bit by surprise. Jesus was exploring some independence at age 12, and apparently knew an impressive amount of Scripture because he was able to teach adults in the Temple about the principles it contained. He knew enough, according to Luke, to astonish learned men. Since his own parents were surprised by what he was saying about doing his Father's business, it makes sense to assume that this was not behavior they were yet accustomed to.

The Son of God was leaving boyhood behind, and stepping out onto a larger stage. Within his family he was apparently trustworthy enough so that neither parent was very obsessive about where he was or might have been doing, since they left town without checking too closely on him. Luke says that when this happened, Jesus knew who his Father was and was already connected to his mission. Those are all pretty impressive qualities to exhibit at only twelve years old. Luke's short account of twelve-year-old Jesus in the temple makes it clear that Jesus was destined for greater things; but that last phrase in verse 49 about how he treated his parents kinda sneaks up on you. **"He was obedient to them."** In our own walk with God, 1 Samuel 15:22 reminds us that "to obey is better than sacrifice, and to hearken than the fat of rams." God values obedience. Apparently even the King of Kings obeyed his mom and dad. Young people take note: If God with skin on obeyed his parents, so should you.

The Boy Who Obeyed His Parents

Our culture loves the shallow things,
And all the toys celebrity brings:
The bling, the cars, the diamond rings,
The cash register when it cha-chings!
But Luke said Jesus knew the ways
Of wisdom far beyond his days,
And taught adults who were amazed!
So, Jesus grew up mentally,
And physically, and socially.
He also grew up spiritually,
In ways you could and could not see.
You'd think that Jesus had it made,
The power of God in man displayed--
And yet the hand that Jesus played
Was this: The Son of God obeyed.
He didn't try to take command,
He didn't overplay his hand,
But followed what His Father planned:
Obey. Be humble. Understand
That life in all its parts can be much greater than the sum;
And greatness doesn't celebrate before its hour is come.
The key to life is not what's most expedient,
But this: know what God wants, and be obedient.

31 The Christmas Story

December 31   Your Testimony: Is There Enough Evidence to Convict?

The Christmas season always has so much meaning to me that I hate to see it end. I know it's partly because it's a story filled with humility and surprise, with unexpected details that validate the arrival of a long-awaited king. And it's also amazing because it's a yearly reminder that Jesus was a REAL person who was born and walked among us.

The arrival of Jesus was witnessed by shepherds and magi, by inn keepers and angels. Men recalled Scriptures from long ago and quoted them while celebrating the birth of Jesus; surprisingly, they still do today! Why do so many people commemorate his life every year? We're a long way from first century Judea, and there is so much legend and commercialism today around the Christmas baby Jesus it might be easy to forget who he was and what he did.

Lest the story seem ancient and quaint, I thought it would be good to play "Eyewitness News" in the gospel accounts of his early ministry and get some first-hand statements from people who were there, who saw Jesus, talked with him, and witnessed what he did. The story of the baby Jesus reminds us how he came to earth; the things he did as a man reveal WHY he came to earth.

One of the early reporters was his cousin, John the Baptist, who said this: "I indeed baptize you with water unto repentance: but he that cometh after me is mightier than I, whose shoes I am not worthy to bear: he shall baptize you with the Holy Ghost, and with fire..." (Matthew 3:11 KJV) And this: "Again the next day after John stood, and two of his disciples; And looking upon Jesus as he walked, he said, Behold the Lamb of God!" (John 1:35-36 KJV) Before Jesus ever drove money-changers from the temple or performed a miracle, and before his wisdom changed the way everyone looked at religion, John identified him as a game-changer. Long before the cross, and long before Jesus said, "This is my body", John pointed to Jesus as the Lamb of God, the sacrifice who would take away the sins of the world.

This Christmas season, we've celebrated the birth of the baby Jesus, the newborn king. Let's not forget who he grew up to be. Christmas may begin in a manger, but it ends on a cross. Reliable witnesses provided proof of Jesus' birth; they also remind us throughout the Gospels that we should celebrate his life as well! If a reliable eyewitness account can get someone convicted of murder, perhaps we should allow a few good eyewitness accounts to get us convicted about God's love and the way he showed us how to live...

Jesus didn't change the world simply because he was born; he somehow changed the hearts of men in ways that stirred love, humility, service, and courage. Peter was transformed from an impetuous coward to a bold leader. John became obsessed with the love of God. Matthew forsook his wealth and wrote a Gospel. Thomas believed. Paul was transformed from being a zealous persecutor of the church to one of its most ardent missionaries. There are hundreds of first-century testimonies about Jesus, and they all speak to his power to transform; but it doesn't stop there. Even today, people will testify about the life-changing love of Jesus Christ. I'm one of them. Jesus has changed my life, and I'd love to tell you all about it sometime. If it's not handy for you to talk to me, then go to IAMSECOND.com and listen. Dozens and even hundreds of testimonies offer valid evidence that Christmas celebrates the birth of the Son of God, the Messiah, Jesus Christ. Every Christmas reminds us that wise men still seek him.

Living Proof (As one of the shepherds might have said, years later...)

I saw him there, your Honor, in the manger where he lay;
I saw him in the village, with the other kids at play.
He taught there in the temple court when he was just a lad;
The elders were astonished at the questions that he had!
I saw him heal the sick and lame, and heard him preach and teach,
While hundreds fed on fish and bread extended from his reach.
I swear, Your Honor, on my oath that every word is true;
That many people heard his words and saw what he could do—
I'm sure you would believe in Him if you had seen him too!

Thank you for reading through these devotionals with me. I hope you have an awesome New Year, and that you celebrate the true Spirit of Christmas each and every day! Please feel free to visit my blog at BoJackson54.com

Index to Scripture References

18   John 1:14; 14:6

19   Luke 2:1-4; John 7:41-42
20   Luke 2:8-10
21   Luke 2:8, 15, 20; Matthew 2:11
22   Matthew 2:1-3, 7-8
23   Matthew 2:4-6, 16-18
24   Matthew 2:9-12
        Matthew 2:11; John 3:16; Romans 5:15; 6:23; Ephesians
25   2:8-9
26   Matthew 2:12-15; Ephesians 6:12
27   Matthew 2:19-23
28   Luke 2:51-52
29   Luke 2:42-50; Mark 3:21, 31; 6:3
30   Luke 2:49-51
31   Matthew 3:11; John 1:35-36

ABOUT THE AUTHOR

Bo Jackson is a husband, father, and grandfather who enjoys exploring the Word of God and applying it to his own life. He has been a long-time Sunday school teacher, and was also active in Young Life as a volunteer leader for many years. He writes a daily blog at BoJackson54.com and on his Facebook page as The Original Bo Jackson.

You can find his other Devotional books, *Beggar's Bread* and *Slaying Giants: Thirty Days With David* on Amazon.com

Made in the
USA
Lexington, KY